W9-DBT-367

FLOORS AND STAIRWAYS

TIME
LIFE
BOOKS

This volume is part of a series offering home
owners detailed instructions on repairs,
construction and improvements which they can
undertake themselves.

HOME REPAIR
AND IMPROVEMENT

FLOORS AND STAIRWAYS

BY THE EDITORS OF
TIME-LIFE BOOKS

TIME-LIFE BOOKS
AMSTERDAM

TIME-LIFE BOOKS

EUROPEAN EDITOR: Kit van Tulleken
Assistant European Editor: Gillian Moore
Design Director: Ed Skyner
Photography Director: Pamela Marke
Chief of Research: Vanessa Kramer
Chief Sub-Editor: Ilse Gray

HOME REPAIR AND IMPROVEMENT

EDITORIAL STAFF FOR FLOORS AND STAIRWAYS
Editor: William Frankel
Assistant Editor: Stuart Gannes
Designer: Anne Masters
Picture Editor: Adrian Allen
Associate Designer: Kenneth E. Hancock
Text Editors: Willim H. Forbis, Jim Hicks, Brian
McGinn, Ellen Philips, Mark M. Steele
Staff Writers: Thierry Bright-Sagnier, Stephen Brown,
Steven J. Forbis, Lee Greene, Lydia Preston, Brooke C.
Stoddard, David Thiemann
Art Associates: George Bell, Michelle Clay, Mary
Louise Mooney, Dale Pollekoff, Lorraine Rivard,
Richard Whiting
Editorial Assistant: Eleanor G. Kask

EUROPEAN EDITION
Series Director: Jackie Matthews
Text Editor: Charles Boyle
Editors: Margaret Hall (principal), Christopher
Farman
Designer: Paul Reeves
Sub-Editors: Wendy Gibbons, Hilary Hockman

EDITORIAL PRODUCTION
Production Assistants: Nikki Allen, Maureen Kelly
Picture Co-ordinator: Peggy Tout
Editorial Department: Theresa John, Debra Lelliott

THE CONSULTANTS: Leslie Stokes was a self-employed carpenter and joiner
for seven years, specializing in purpose-made joinery and internal
fittings. Since 1976 he has taught in the building department at the
Hammersmith and West London College.

Alan Bayliss served his apprenticeship with a leading Sydney cabinet-
making firm. He worked as a carpenter and cabinet-maker for 18 years,
then took a Diploma in Teaching from Sydney College of Advanced
Education. Since 1970 he has been a teacher of cabinet-making at Sydney
Technical College.

Victor M. Casamento is an independent builder who designs and
constructs custom homes in the U.S.A.

Roswell W. Ard is a consulting structural engineer and a professional
home inspector in the U.S.A. He has written professional papers on wood-
frame construction techniques.

R. Daniel Nicholson Jr. is an assistant production manager and estimator
for a Washington, D.C., home remodelling service.

Contents

1 Restoring Damaged Floors

Getting down to the grain. A whirling strip of abrasive paper in a belt sander removes old finish from a timber floor at floor-to-wall corners, where a large drum sander cannot reach. You will need to sand the floor three times—first with coarse, then with medium, then with fine abrasive paper—to expose the natural texture of the wood.

Contemporary floor and staircase construction is a synthesis of time-proven designs with modern materials and installation techniques. Pre-finished and prefabricated materials make it surprisingly easy to improve a house by installing or restoring floors of gleaming wood or tile, sturdy concrete or soft carpet. Hired professional tools can help with the big jobs, such as laying a new concrete slab, fitting carpets or building a staircase; synthetic adhesives, floor finishes and concrete additives make the repair of tile and concrete, once a task for professionals, an everyday affair.

Perhaps the most basic of modern flooring materials is chipboard, a combination of wood particles and resin, bonded under heat and high pressure. Strong and virtually unwarpable, it provides a firm base for any floor from basement to attic. Laid over concrete *(pages 36–37)*, it makes a warm base for finish flooring; over joists, it is as strong as traditional timber floorboards, and much simpler to install. It is a good base for hard tiles or resilient floor coverings and, combined with insulating material, makes an economical soundproof floor.

For a new staircase, you can order a prefabricated traditional staircase, a space-saving spiral stair or a disappearing staircase for a loft or attic that can be installed in a few hours. Alternatively, you can build a simple flight of stairs from scratch *(pages 86–89)*, using an electric router to cut out the housings for the treads. This can be hired, along with a variety of tools used for the installation and restoration of flooring. A portable concrete mixer, for example, will eliminate hours of backbreaking labour; knee-kickers *(page 108)* are essential tools for stretching woven or hessian-backed carpets smooth and tight; and adjustable props enable you to make the large structural repairs which were once left to professionals.

Any flooring from attic to basement needs occasional maintenance and repair. Floors are intimately linked to the structure of a house, and natural shifts in the structure put stress on them. Other enemies of floors are moisture, abuse and age. Whatever the cause of the damage, repairs are usually possible. Some are major projects—to replace the supports beneath a sagging floor, for example *(pages 18–21)*, you will have to enlist helpers—but most require only the right materials and a few professional tricks. An accurately placed nail or wedge may be all that is needed. You can replace or tighten worn or loose flooring *(pages 8–13)* or sand yellowed or stained wood, then refinish the floor with permanently transparent polyurethane *(pages 22–25)*. New adhesives ease the repair of resilient flooring *(pages 26–29)*, and new bonding agents simplify the resurfacing of concrete floors.

Quick Cures for a Timber Floor's Ailments

Although timber, the most common flooring material, is one of the most durable, it can crack, stain and burn. Fixings can also work loose, causing the floorboards to squeak and sag. Fortunately, the remedies for all these ailments are simple. Cracks can be filled, stains and burns sanded away and loose boards retightened. In the event of serious damage, you can replace your boards without leaving any surgical scars.

Most squeaks arise from flooring that is no longer firmly attached to the joists below. Where the floorboards also serve as the ceiling for an unfinished basement, ask someone to walk on the floor while you stand below and watch for movement over the joists. The squeak can then be eliminated by inserting timber wedges into the gaps between joists and boards *(opposite page, above)*. Where the underside of the floor is inaccessible, refasten loose boards to the joists from above; cut floor brads may cause the boards to split and can themselves work loose, so use countersunk screws *(page 10, above)*. If the boards have been secret-nailed and there is no visible clue to the position of the joists, you will have to lift a board to locate them.

Squeaks can also result from rubbing between adjacent boards. Ask someone to walk over the noisy area while you watch for play in the floor and feel for vibrations. If you are not going to cover the boards, first try remedies that do not mar the finished surface: force powdered graphite, talcum powder or wooden wedges into the joints *(opposite page, below)*. Should these solutions fail, secure the boards from above with countersunk screws.

Even more common than squeaks are cracks arising from humidity and temperature changes, which cause boards to shrink unevenly. Such cracks can be plugged with thin wooden strips or with a paste made from sawdust and floor finish. Use sawdust from some out-of-the-way section of the floor, such as the corner of a built-in cupboard. Work 4 parts sawdust and 1 part finish into a thick paste and pack into the crack *(page 24)*.

Surface defects, such as stains and burns, can be erased by sanding if they do not go too deep. To determine the extent of the damage, go over the blemished area with a wood scraper. If the defect starts to lift out, the board can be saved by refinishing. Otherwise, it must be prised out of the floor and replaced *(pages 11–13)*.

When replacing floorboards, inspect for decay in the surrounding timber. Probe boards and joists with a bradawl or screwdriver and examine the wood for pinhead-sized holes—a sure sign of wood-boring beetle. If the timber feels spongy or cracks down or across the grain, rot has set in and you should seek professional advice. Lightly decayed floors can be treated, but severely damaged boards must be replaced.

While you are surveying the floor, check that the bridging is not decayed or inadequate—it should provide reinforcement for all joist spans of 3.5 metres or more. A floor that also serves as a basement ceiling can be reinforced with new bridging from below; if the joists are not accessible, you will have to remove floorboards and work from above *(page 10, below)*. The bridging should fit tightly between the joists. As these may be unevenly spaced, measure between each pair of joists and cut individual blocks accordingly.

Anatomy of a timber floor. A suspended timber floor consists of two layers: a supporting base of parallel timber joists and a covering of timber boards or sheets of man-made board such as chipboard. Nowadays, the boards are mostly tongue and groove, but in older houses they may be square edged—a type sometimes laid diagonally for greater stability. At ground level, the joists are usually 100 by 50 mm timbers spaced at 400 mm centres. They are supported by sleeper walls built up from a layer of oversite concrete or, in the case of older houses, by sleeper walls and outside walls combined.

For upper floors and ground-level floors above basements *(right)*, the joists have to span greater distances between walls. Standard 200 to 225 by 50 mm upper joists will span up to 3.5 metres; for uninterrupted spans greater than this, timber or steel beams are sometimes installed beneath them to provide intermediate support *(pages 18–21)*. The ends of the joists are either built into the walls or supported by metal holders called joist hangers. Midway across their span, the joists may be braced to prevent the wood from twisting as it ages. Two types of bracing are used: herringbone bridging, which consists of pairs of timbers fixed diagonally between the joists, and solid bridging which is made up of single blocks *(right)*.

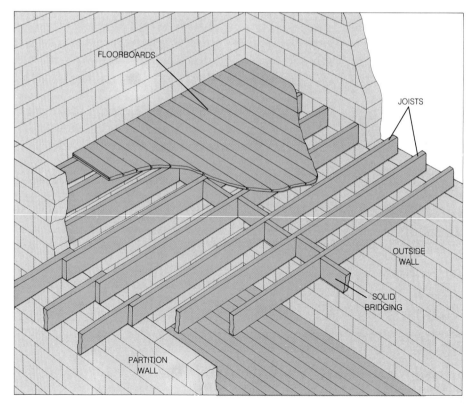

Eliminating Squeaks

Wedging boards from below. Carefully hammer a timber wedge between the joists and the loose boards to prevent movement. Do not force the boards upwards or you may cause them to become higher than the rest of the floor.

Wedging boards from above. To stop floorboards from rubbing together, force wooden wedges into the joints between the boards. Use a hammer and either a nail punch or a small piece of scrap metal to tap the wedges into place. Insert one wedge every 150 mm until the squeak is eliminated.

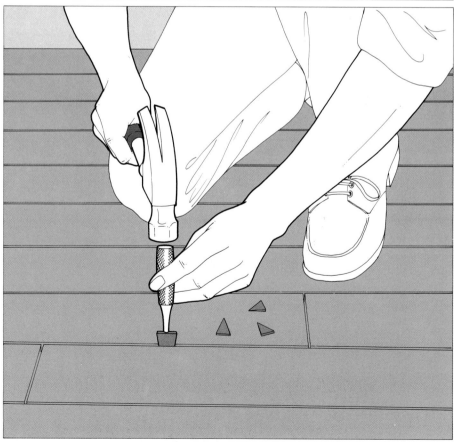

Securing boards from above. Drill pairs of pilot holes into the creaking boards above each joist, and secure the boards to the joists using 37 mm No. 8 countersunk screws. Angle the screws towards each other to grip the boards tightly to the joists. Cover the screw heads with wood filler, allow the filler to dry and sand smooth.

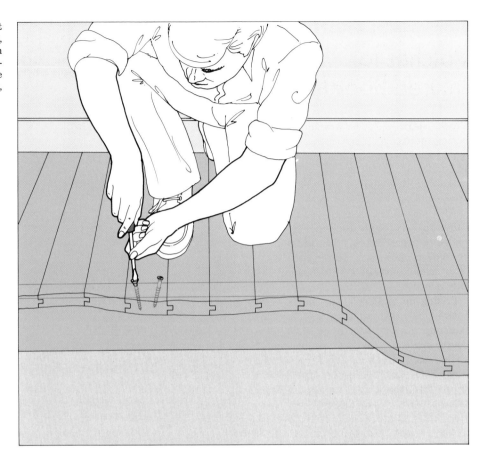

Reinforcing the Joists

Installing solid bridging. Snap a chalk line across the joists, midway along their span. Cut timber blocks to fit tightly between the joists, using timber the same thickness and either the same depth or 25 mm less if you need to allow room for underfloor pipes or cables. Working across the room, position the blocks on alternate sides of the chalk line and secure them at each end with two 100 mm round-wire nails driven through the joists. Where a block adjoins the wall, you need fix from the joist side only.

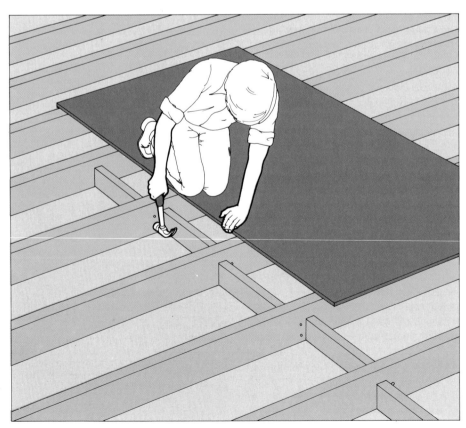

Made-to-Measure Patches for Injured Boards

Cracks, stains, rot and infestation by wood-boring insects can all weaken or mar the appearance of timber floorboards. If you intend covering the boards with carpet, tiles or another wood surface, the appearance is not important and, once the damaged boards have been removed, a patch of chipboard can easily be cut to size and nailed in place. To enjoy the original timber surface, however, replacement boards of matching width and thickness are the only solution.

Prising up and replacing square-edged boards is relatively straightforward. Patching an area of tongue and groove floorboards laid directly over joists, as described on these three pages, takes more time. Before the damaged boards can be prised from the joists, the tongue of one board must be cut off *(Step 1)*. A flooring saw, with its curved, toothed end, is made for this job, but a pencil-thin padsaw or the more familiar tenon saw can also be used. Because you are sawing "blind", disconnect any electrical circuits entering the room and proceed carefully, stop if you encounter any resistance that might indicate underfloor pipes or cables.

If your boards are so tightly wedged that you cannot insert a bolster or saw blade into the joints, make several cuts along the length of one board with a circular saw set to slightly less than the board's thickness. Complete these splits with a bolster, then prise up the separate pieces. Use the same technique for removing hardwood strips nailed to a subfloor.

All tongue and groove boards may be either face-nailed—in which case the nail heads will be visible on the surface of the boards—or secret-nailed, with the nails driven at an angle through the tongue of each board and concealed by the groove of the adjacent board. If the floor is secret-nailed, damaged boards must be sawn across alongside the edge of a joist, then cut across the centre of the joist with a chisel *(Steps 2 and 3)*. Using this method, the saw blade will not be damaged by the hidden nails. If the floor is face-nailed, punch the nails through the boards and then saw the boards carefully over the joists.

1 **Splitting the tongue of a damaged board.** Insert a bolster between two of the damaged boards and strike it with a hammer to split the tongue. Then insert the blade of a flooring saw into the slit and continue cutting the tongue between the boards, working along the length of the damaged area and reverting to the bolster if you have to cut over a joist. Directly above the inner edges of the joists that frame the damaged area, square a line across the boards.

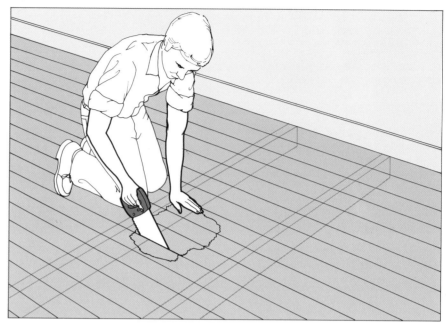

2 **Cutting across the grain.** Determine the thickness of the boards by splitting the tongue of one of the damaged boards over a joist, then inserting a knife blade, a thin screwdriver or the end of a metal rule between the boards. With a circular saw set to exactly this depth, saw the damaged boards across the grain along the lines which you have marked at the edges of the joists *(Step 1)*. Then, with a wood chisel, make a straight cut across the grain of the boards over the centre of the joists at both ends of the damaged area of floor.

3 **Prising out the damaged boards.** Insert a bolster between the boards with the split tongue, near where you have sawn across the grain. Prise up the first board by forcing the bolster away from you, using your foot if necessary. As the board begins to angle upwards, work along its length towards the joist at the other end of the damaged section. When you have removed the section of board between the joists, cut back to the lines cut across the centres of the joists with a chisel. Remove nails with pincers or a claw hammer. Prise and chisel off the rest of the damaged boards in the same way.

4 **Inserting a new section of board.** Cut a length of floorboard to replace one you have removed and slide it into position, fitting its grooved edge over the tongue of the preceding course. Force the new board tightly into position by slotting the groove of a scrap piece of board over its tongue and then striking the scrap board with a mallet.

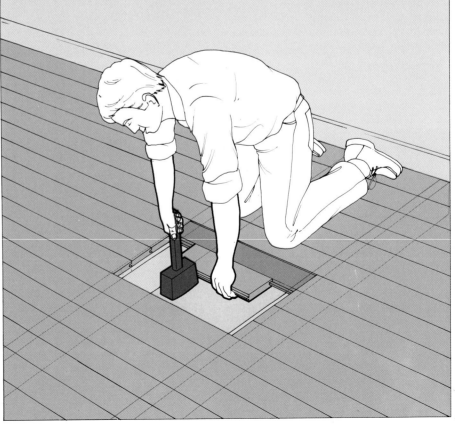

5 **Secret-nailing a board.** Drive 32 mm lost-head nails at a 45-degree angle through the base of the tongue of the replacement board and into the joists *(inset)*. Use one nail per joist, and punch them into the board with a nail punch. Fit and secure all the replacement floorboards, except the last one, in the same way.

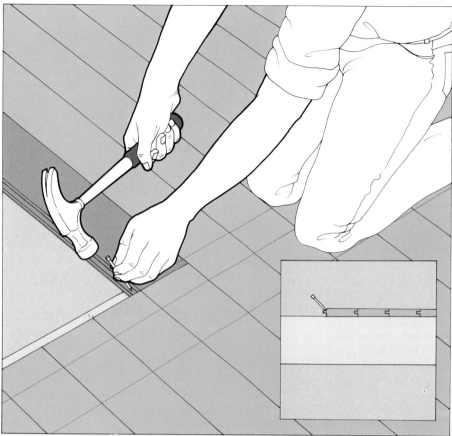

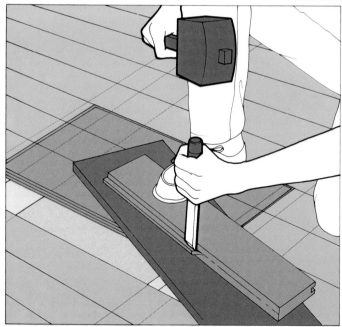

6 **Inserting the last board.** To enable the final replacement board to be fitted, turn it upside down on a scrap piece of timber and remove the lower lip of the groove with a mallet and chisel *(above)*. Then fit the board in position and gently tap it home with a mallet, protecting its surface with a scrap of wood.

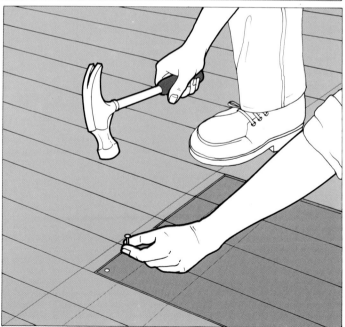

7 **Face-nailing the last board.** Secure the last board with lost-head or oval nails two and a half times the thickness of the floorboards in length. Use two nails per joist, driving them in about 10 mm from the edges of the board. Punch the nails below the surface of the floor and cover them with a wood filler tinted to match the boards.

Supports That Bolster a Sagging Floor

Sagging floors usually occur in older houses. Over the years, joists have bowed from overloading, supporting walls have crumbled and subsidence has caused walls to drop or dip. Old-fashioned construction methods placed joist ends and wall plates (the timber beams on which joists rested at exterior walls) in direct contact with potentially damp masonry, creating an ideal environment for wood-rotting fungi and wood-boring insects. In addition, before the days of strict building regulations, it was easy to cut corners and install joists which were too small for the weight which they would have to support. The overloaded joists eventually sagged with the strain.

In modern houses, ground-floor joists are usually supported by low sleeper walls and protected by a damp-proof course. Poor practices, however, can still escape the notice of building inspectors. Joists may even be installed upside down, with a slightly bowed edge facing downwards, which can cause any subsequent sagging of the joists to show up even more.

The repair for a sag depends upon its cause, and your first task is diagnosis. Inspect the framework underneath the floor for faulty construction (below). Where ceilings prevent easy access to the joists, it is usually simpler to work from above, removing a few floorboards for your preliminary examination (pages 11–13). Test for rot and insect damage (page 8), and treat small areas of decay with a preservative. A large sag occurring in conjunction with seemingly unrelated problems such as cracked plaster, leaky plumbing or doors that stick, may well be a sign of structural damage, in which case you should seek the advice of a professional.

Slight dips in the floor can be repaired in the same way that you would repair a squeak, with timber wedges driven between a joist and the floor (page 9). A larger sag is a symptom of real trouble, requiring the straightening and strengthening of one or more joists by doubling—that is, by bolting new joists to the weak ones (pages 16–17). Joists that have rotted through must be replaced (page 16). Before starting either job, make sure that pipes, electrical wires and hot air ducts will not prevent you from slipping the new joists into place. If there are many obstructions, you will have to move them or get a professional to do it for you.

In some cases it may be easier to install a rolled steel joist (RSJ) than to shore up failed joists individually (pages 18–21). An RSJ is a permanent support that runs beneath the centre of a span of joists, taking all of the weight off weakened or overloaded timber.

Whatever solution you decide upon—doubling, replacing or installing an RSJ—you will first have to straighten the floor with one or more adjustable props. These telescoping metal posts fitted with plates at the base and top can be hired from builders' merchants or a tool-hire company, and their screw threads should be greased before you begin work.

The demonstration opposite shows a prop being positioned in a basement; for upper floors, you will first have to strip off the ceiling to expose the joists. For a very low space under a ground floor, hire a screw jack—a squat, bell-shaped prop with a screw that can be extended upwards about 300 mm (opposite page, below).

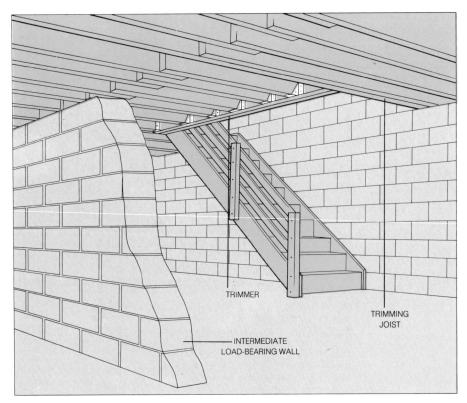

TRIMMER

TRIMMING JOIST

INTERMEDIATE LOAD-BEARING WALL

Why floors sag. This drawing shows the horizontal and vertical supports that carry the weight of the ground floor above a basement. Beneath the floor are two spans of joists, laid in parallel rows. The outer ends of the joists are notched into the exterior walls of the house; their inner ends rest on an intermediate load-bearing wall.

Shifts in the positions of these parts can cause sags in the floor above. A damaged or crumbling supporting wall will undermine the entire structure. The trimmers and trimming joists that frame the stairwell carry extra weight and must either be doubled or made of thicker timber than the other joists (pages 78–81). Any of the timber members could be weakened by rot or wood-boring insects. Where joists come into direct contact with an exterior masonry wall, there is a danger of damp penetrating and rotting the wood; the ends of any new joists installed in this way must be treated with preservative to prevent decay. Finally, notches and holes can weaken timber. Pipes or cables that pass through joists should be positioned near the wall and at the centre or top, never at the bottom, of a joist.

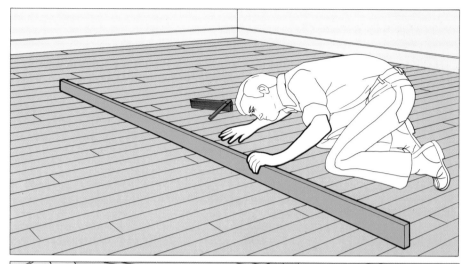

Propping Up a Floor

Measuring a ground floor sag. Lay a long piece of straight-edged timber across the sagging area, at right angles to the floorboards. Measure the gap between the straightedge and the floor and mark the floor where the sag is deepest.

Measure from the mark on the floor to two different reference points—walls or stairways, for example—that lie at right angles to each other and that also appear in the basement. In the basement, take measurements from the reference points to position the prop.

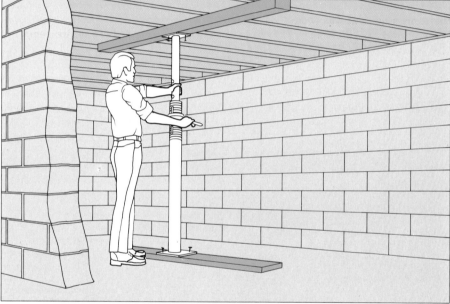

Propping from a basement. Position an adjustable prop beneath the joist that needs straightening, resting its base plate on a length of 225 by 50 mm timber. Crank the prop up until its top plate is about 100 mm below the sagging joist, then rest a 100 by 75 mm supporting beam, about 1.5 metres long, on the top plate at right angles to the joists. Remove any strutting or bridging between joists that are spanned by the supporting beam. Slowly crank up the prop until the floor above is perfectly straight.

Propping in a small space. Directly beneath the sagging joist, set a screw jack between a timber board and a supporting beam, following the instructions above for using an adjustable prop. Turn the screw of the jack until the beam presses against the joists. In many cases, the jack will not rise from the floor to the joists even when fully extended. To raise the base of a jack, set its pad on a pyramidal framework called cribwork, made of rough 150 mm-square structural-grade timber. Stack the beams in parallel pairs, with each pair at right angles to the one beneath it; the top pair of beams should be about 450 mm apart.

Raise the jack gradually until the sag in the joist disappears.

Help for Weakened Joists

Once it is evident that a damaged or overloaded joist needs repair, decide whether to double it or to replace it. Doubling assumes that there is still some useful strength left in the old joist, which is straightened and bolted in place beside a new one. Replacing is the only solution for a joist that is rotten or badly cracked.

For both doubling and replacing joists, use straight, structural-grade timber, free from splits or large knots and pressure-treated to protect it against attack from rot or wood-boring insects.

The new joist should match the depth and thickness of the existing joists and be 200 mm longer than the span between the walls—this allows for 100 mm at each end to be supported by an intermediate load-bearing wall or bedded within an exterior wall. If the narrow edges of the new joist are slightly bowed—check by sighting along the crown—install it with the convex edge uppermost.

The method for doubling joists shown on these pages calls for 125 by 12 mm coach bolts and for timber connectors, sharply toothed discs that grip the inner surfaces of the doubled joists and prevent them from slipping. To replace a joist, first make sure that there is no heavy object—a piano or a washing machine—immediately above. Then saw a section at least 150 mm wide from the middle of the old joist and prise it down with a crowbar. Prise away the two end pieces, working them loose from the walls with a chisel. Extract protruding floorboard nails with pincers or, if you intend to resurface the floor, knock the nails back up with a hammer. With a bolster, slightly enlarge the holes in the wall where the old joist was bedded. Position, prop and bed the new joist in the wall using the same techniques as are shown here for doubling a joist.

1 Making a hole for a new joist. Using a club hammer and a bolster, chop a hole 100 mm deep into the outer wall next to the joist which is to be doubled. Make the hole slightly larger than the actual joist dimensions. If the other end of the new joist is also to be bedded in a wall, cut another hole similar to the first one but at least 100 mm deeper. Wear gloves and goggles while you are making these holes to protect yourself from flying chippings.

2 Inserting the joist. With an assistant, lift the new joist into position. If one end is to rest on a supporting wall, simply slide the other end into place beside the old joist in the outer wall (*above*). If both ends are to be bedded in walls, angle one end into the deeper hole, push it as far as it will go, then lift the other end until it is level with the old joist and shift it across into the other hole. At least 100 mm of a joist bedded in a wall must be supported by masonry.

Following the techniques described on page 15, support both the old and new joists with an adjustable prop. Raise the prop until both joists touch the floorboards above, or, if you are correcting a sagging joist, until the floor above is perfectly level.

WASHER

TIMBER CONNECTOR

3 **Connecting the joists.** With an electric drill fitted with a spade bit or a brace and bit, drill holes 13 mm in diameter through both the old joist and the new one. Drill the first hole as near to the wall as possible, then space the holes at 450 mm intervals, half way between the top and bottom of the joists *(above)*. Separate the joists with a screwdriver or crowbar, then slot washers on to the bolts and push them through the holes in one of the joists. Place a timber connector over the end of each bolt between the joists and push the bolts through the second joist *(inset)*. Clamp the joists together at each bolt with a G-cramp so that the teeth of the connectors are forced into the timber. Then slip a second washer over each of the bolts and tightly fasten the nuts.

4 **Making good.** When the end of the new joist is bedded in a wall, wedge pieces of slate or tile into the gap underneath the joist to give it a solid footing. With a pointing trowel *(left)*, pack round the end of the joist with a strong, stiff mortar—5 parts sand to 1 part Portland cement. Allow the mortar to dry for at least 48 hours before removing the prop. Replace any bridging which was removed before doubling the joist with solid bridging *(page 10)*.

Straightening a Floor with a Steel Joist

Installing a rolled steel joist (RSJ) under an entire span of sagging joists may seem a daunting prospect. In reality, although this is indeed heavy work, it is considerably less laborious than the task of doubling or replacing several individual joists across the span.

Ask a builders' merchant or your building control officer to help you select a joist of the right size and strength; a common standard size is 203 by 102 mm, but for wide rooms a larger size may be necessary. It is a wise precaution to submit plans of the work you propose to your local authority. You will have to comply with fire regulations; an unprotected steel joist twists in extreme heat. In living areas the RSJ must be boxed in with plaster on an expanded metal lath or with plasterboard nailed to a timber framework *(page 21)*. This cladding also serves to conceal the RSJ and make it less obtrusive. As rolled steel is inclined to rust, paint the RSJ with rustproofer before it is installed.

Because of the heavy weight that an RSJ supports, its ends must be bedded in load-bearing walls. Exterior walls are ideal; if you are in any doubt as to the suitability of an intermediate wall, you should consult a building surveyor or structural engineer who will be able to give you expert advice. It is also important to consider the weight of the RSJ itself—about 25 kilograms per metre. For safety and efficiency, enlist the help of two or more assistants, depending on the length of the RSJ, to raise it into position; one person per metre is a useful calculation to bear in mind.

While the RSJ is being installed, the weight of the floor above is transferred through the adjustable props to the floor, or floors, below. The situation portrayed on these pages is an ideal one: a solid basement floor takes all the weight and no further propping is necessary. But where you are working in an upstairs room, you must support each of the floors below you with adjustable props, positioned directly underneath each other, right down to a solid footing on the ground.

1 **Straightening the joists.** Measure the sag in the floor and locate its lowest point on the joists below, as described on page 15. At about 600 mm from either side of this mark, install pairs of adjustable props *(page 15, centre)*, each pair supporting a beam long enough to span all the sagging joists. Raise the props gradually, a little at a time, until a straightedge on the floor above indicates that the sag has disappeared. Then raise the props a further few millimetres.

2 Preparing bearings for the RSJ. At a point midway along the span of joists that need reinforcing, use a bolster and club hammer to chop a hole in an exterior wall at least 100 mm in depth and slightly larger than the cross-sectional dimensions of the RSJ. The top of the hole must be level with the lower edges of the propped-up joists, and the bottom must be aligned with a mortar course so that the RSJ will rest on a level surface. At the opposite side of the propped-up span of joists, cut a matching hole into an exterior wall or completely through a load-bearing wall. Ensure that at least one of the holes is deep enough to allow you to lift the RSJ into place *(page 16)*.

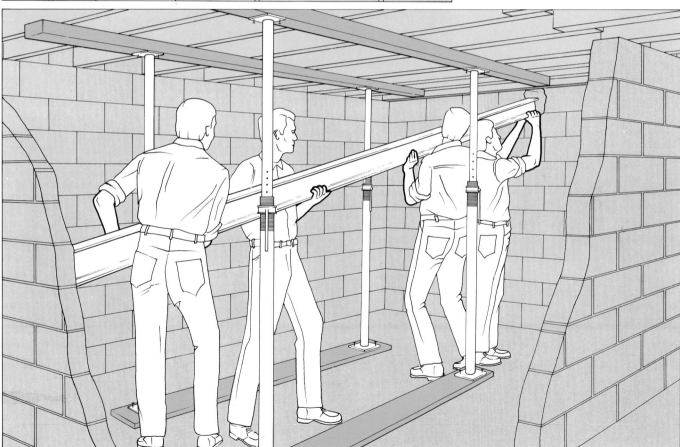

3 Installing the RSJ. With the assistance of two or more helpers, raise one end of the RSJ and place it in the deeper of the bearing holes. Push it right to the back of the hole, then raise the other end and slide the RSJ across into the hole opposite. It is essential that both ends of the RSJ rest on secure masonry bearings at least 100 mm deep. If an intermediate load-bearing wall serves as one of the bearings, push the first end of the RSJ through the hole in the wall, then slide the other end across and into the recess you have prepared in the exterior wall.

4 **Levelling the RSJ.** Use adjustable props to raise the RSJ until its top is level with the underside of the straightened joists, wedging pieces of slate or tile into the gaps beneath the ends of the RSJ. If you have had to cut away a substantial amount of masonry in order to reach a level bearing, raise the ends of the RSJ with pieces of brick.

5 **Inserting wedges.** Check with a spirit level that the RSJ is horizontal, and adjust where necessary by inserting fragments of slate and tile at the bearings. Where joists do not come in contact with the RSJ, drive in hardwood folding wedges *(inset)* to make up the gap.

JOIST

FOLDING
WEDGES

RSJ

6 **Making good at the walls.** Mix a strong mortar—5 parts sand to 1 part Portland cement—with just enough water for a stiff but workable consistency. Pack it into the spaces around the ends of the RSJ with a pointing trowel, making sure that all slates, tiles or bricks you have used as filling are thoroughly embedded. Allow the mortar at least 48 hours to cure before removing the props.

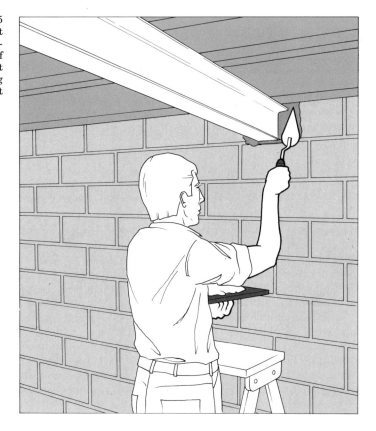

Cladding a Steel Joist for an Upstairs Room

Enclosing an RSJ in plasterboard. Construct two ladder-shaped frameworks—known as cradling—out of 37 by 37 mm battens. Make each "ladder" as long as the RSJ and as wide as the RSJ is deep, securing the "rungs" at 400 mm centres with 75 mm wire nails. Butt the frames against the sides of the RSJ and secure them to the joists with 63 mm No. 8 screws. After attaching a plasterboard ceiling to the joists, nail to the battens a boxing of 12 mm plasterboard, installing the bottom section first.

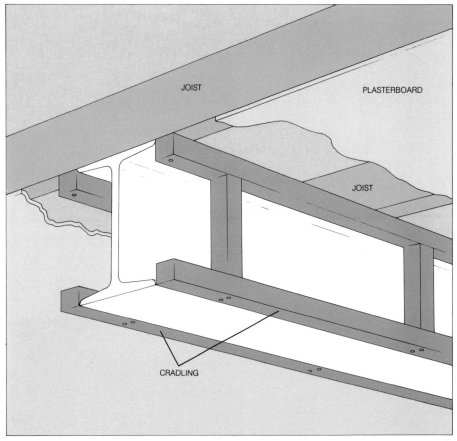

JOIST

PLASTERBOARD

JOIST

CRADLING

Putting a New Face on an Old Timber Floor

Your varnished timber floors are so worn and scuffed that no amount of waxing and polishing will restore their gloss. Or perhaps you have decided to expose the natural texture and grain of a painted floor. In either case, you must refinish your floors. It is a four-stage job: sanding off the old finish, bleaching out stains, filling any gaps in the wood and applying a new, durable polyurethane-based finish *(overleaf)*.

A refinishing job calls for professional equipment, available from most tool-hire shops. You will need a drum sanding machine, in which abrasive paper is fitted over a large revolving cylinder; if you can, hire a machine with a tilt-up lever that lifts the spinning drum from the floor (not all have this feature). In addition, hire a belt or rotary sanding machine for hard-to-get-at areas that the drum sander cannot reach. You will also need goggles and a face mask to block the dust raised by sanding, and ear protectors to deaden the sound of the sander, which is a brutally noisy machine. Finally, to smooth the floor after each successive coat of new finish, hire a professional polishing machine; it polishes with a round pad of fine steel wool.

To help determine the cost of hiring this equipment, estimate the time the job will take—normally, you can sand and finish about 30 square metres of floor in two days. You can economize by completing the work with the sanding machines before you hire the polisher, and use two workers simultaneously, if possible—one to operate the drum sander while the other operates the rotary sanding machine.

You need to use abrasive paper of three grades—coarse, medium and fine. The coarse paper for the first sanding may have any of a variety of grit ratings, depending on the existing surface of the floor. To remove paint or to sand rough floorboards, start with a very coarse, 24-grit paper (the lower the grit rating, the coarser the paper). To remove varnish or shellac, use a 36-grit paper; for parquet floors, use a 60-grit paper. For the second sanding, use a medium, 80-grit paper, and for the final sanding, fine, 100-grit paper.

Have plenty of supplies ready before you begin—at least 10 sheets of abrasive paper and 10 discs of each grade for an average room. You will pay only for the paper you actually use. Be prepared during the job for sudden, unforeseen wastage; a protruding nail head can tear a sheet of abrasive paper to shreds in a split second. Before leaving the hire shop, check that the machines are working, that their dust bags are clean and that you have any special spanners you may need to load the drum sander (get the shop assistant to show you the loading method).

To prepare a room for sanding, remove all the furniture and curtains. If you have underfloor hot-air heating, remove the grilles and cover the vents with polythene. Tighten any loose boards and replace boards that are badly cracked or splintered *(pages 11–13)*. Using a nail punch, drive protruding nail heads 3 mm below the surface of the floor, and to make sanding the edges of the floor easier remove any quadrant moulding from the skirting board *(below)*. Sanding produces highly inflammable dust, so turn off all pilot lights and electrical appliances before you start. Seal doorways into the work area with plastic and open windows for ventilation.

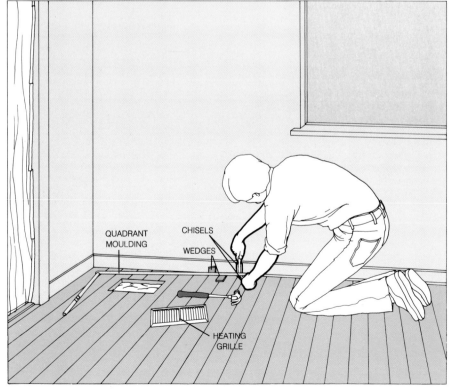

QUADRANT MOULDING

CHISELS

WEDGES

HEATING GRILLE

Sanding Down to the Bare Boards

1 **Removing quadrant moulding.** Beginning at a doorway, and using two sharp chisels a few centimetres apart, gently prise the moulding away from the skirting board and up from the floor. You may have to tap the chisels lightly with a hammer to insert them. When you have loosened about 300 mm of the moulding, slip small wooden wedges behind and under it to prevent it from snapping back into place. Advance along the length of a section of moulding, repeatedly prising out the moulding and moving the wedges. As you remove each section, number it so you will know where to replace it after the job. When all the sections have been removed, pull out any nails that remain in the floor or skirting board.

2 **Loading the drum sander.** With the sander unplugged, thread a sheet of abrasive paper into the loading slot, turn the drum one full revolution and slip the other end of the sheet into the slot; then tighten the paper by turning the nuts at both ends of the drum with the spanners provided by the hire shop. When using fine paper, insert a folded paper wedge of the same grade between the two ends to keep them from slipping out of the slot *(inset)*. Some machines use bands instead of sheets of abrasive paper; the band is inserted from the side of the drum.

ABRASIVE
PAPER WEDGE

LOADING
SLOT

CLAMP NUT

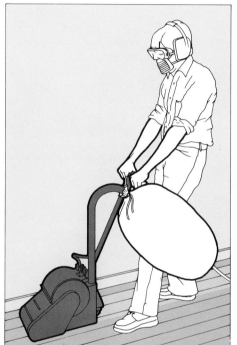

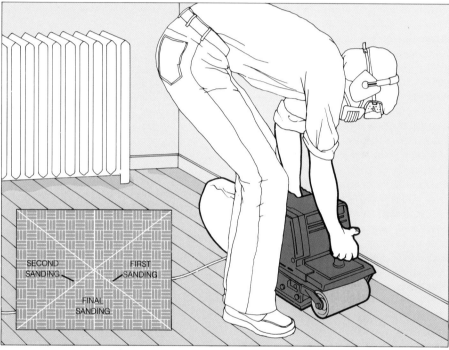

SECOND
SANDING

FIRST
SANDING

FINAL
SANDING

3 **The first sanding.** Tilt the drum from the floor, start the sander, and when the motor reaches full speed lower the drum to the floor and let the machine pull you forwards at a slow, steady pace. Sand a strip or plank floor along the grain of the wood; on parquet floors, which have grains running two ways, do the first sanding in a diagonal direction. When you reach the far wall, raise the drum from the floor, move the cord behind you to one side, then lower the drum and pull the sander backwards over the area you have just sanded. Caution: you must keep the machine in constant motion to prevent it from denting or rippling the wood.

Raise the drum and move the machine to the left or right to overlap the first pass by about 75 mm. Continue forward and backward passes, turning off the machine occasionally to empty the dust bag. When you have sanded the whole width of the room, turn the machine round and sand the strip of floor against the wall.

4 **Second and third sandings.** Load the belt sander with coarse paper and sand the areas missed by the drum sander. Now repeat both the drum and belt sandings, first with medium paper, then with fine. On strip or plank floors, the second and third drum sandings, like the first, should be made with the grain. On parquet floors *(inset)*, do the second sanding on the opposite diagonal to the first, and then the final sanding along the length of the room.

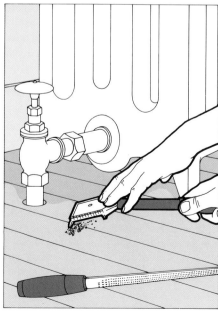

5 **Scraping the tight spots.** In areas that neither the drum nor the belt sander can reach, use a scraper to remove the finish. Always pull the scraper towards you, applying a firm, downward pressure on the tool with both hands, and scrape with the grain wherever possible. Sharpen the scraper blade frequently with a file. To complete this stage of the job, sand the scraped areas by hand.

Two Protective Coats That Seal and Beautify

A new floor finish will last a long time—and so will any blemishes that are visible beneath it. Before applying a finish, check the floor for stains that were not removed by sanding. If you cannot remove them by hand-sanding, use undiluted household bleach. Wearing gloves and goggles, apply a small amount of bleach to the centre of the stain. Wait a few minutes to see how much the bleach lightens the spot, and then apply enough to blend the stained area with the rest of the floor. When you get the right tone, wash the bleached area with warm water and let it dry.

Next, fill any gaps between the floorboards. If the gaps are more than 3 mm you can plug them with long strips of wood at least the same thickness as the existing floorboards. If they are shorter than the floorboards, make sure that they meet on a joist. Gaps smaller than 3 mm can be plugged with wood filler or a sawdust-and-floor-finish paste *(page 8)*.

Then vacuum the floor and go over it with a tack cloth, a rag moistened with turpentine and clear varnish, to pick up all dust before applying the finish.

The easiest finish to apply—and one of the strongest—is polyurethane varnish, made from a synthetic resin that becomes exceptionally tough as it dries and hardens. Polyurethane varnish is available in colourless forms that simply emphasize the grain of the wood, and natural wood hues that alter the shade of the floor. You can also tint clear polyurethane varnish in order to colour the floor—blue or green, for example. These dyes colour the timber but accentuate the grain so that the floor retains the look of wood. Stir the pigment into the varnish before applying.

Traditional finishes—oil-based varnish, shellac, lacquer and wax—yellow with age, wear easily and must be removed when a floor needs refinishing; a polyurethane finish is non-yellowing and far more durable. If it is never waxed, it can be renewed simply by running a polisher loaded with steel wool over the floor and adding another coat of finish.

Plugging the Gaps

Fitting wooden strips. Set a marking gauge to the width of the gap and mark a length of wood with the gauge. Saw the strip slightly oversize, then taper it to form a wedge, using a smoothing plane. Tap the strip into place with a hammer and a block of wood *(below)*. Plane the strip flush with the floor and fix it to any underlying joists with 40 mm panel pins, using a nail punch to punch the pins below the surface.

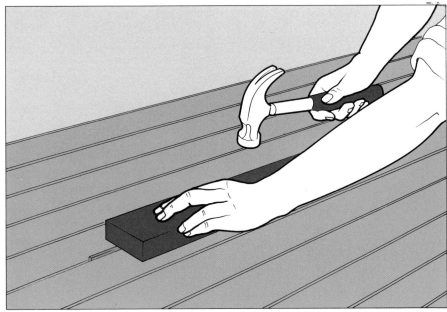

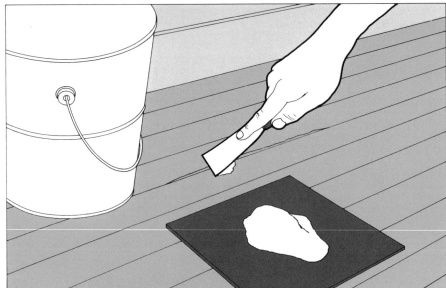

Applying wood filler. Force wood filler into cracks and nail holes with a putty knife. Scrape off any excess filler. When the surface of the filler has dried, hand-sand the filled areas with 100-grit abrasive paper.

2 Filling the hole. To protect the undamaged floor, surround the hole with a border of masking tape at least 25 mm wide and then force the filler firmly into the hole with a putty knife. Scrape off the excess and smooth the surface of the patch with the knife. Let the paste set for 30 minutes; then remove the masking tape and buff the patch with fine steel wool. If the repaired area is duller than the surrounding floor, brush a thin coat of clear nail polish on it.

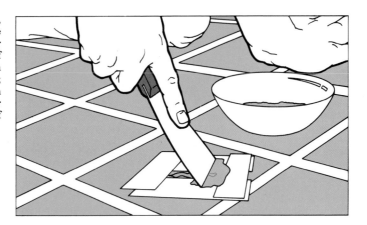

Replacing a Damaged Tile

Removing a tile. For vinyl-asbestos flooring, lay a towel on the tile and warm it with an iron set at medium heat until the adhesive softens and you can lift one corner with a putty knife. Pull up the corner while you slice at the adhesive underneath with the putty knife, reheating the tile with the iron if necessary, until you can remove the entire tile. Wait for the adhesive remaining on the subfloor to become hard—allow about an hour—and then scrape it off.

To remove a damaged vinyl or rubber tile, chip it out with a hammer and chisel, starting at the centre. If you are removing a good vinyl or rubber tile which you intend to re-use, prise up one edge with a chisel and gently chip through adhesive on the underside of the tile. Then scrape off any adhesive remaining on the subfloor.

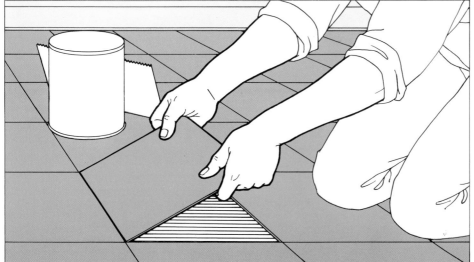

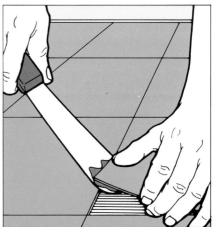

Installing a replacement. Spread a thin layer of adhesive—not more than half the thickness of your tile—on the subfloor with a notched trowel, then butt one edge of the new tile against the edge of an adjoining tile, aligning the pattern. Ease the tile into place. Make sure it is level with surrounding tiles; if it is too high, press it down and quickly wipe off excess adhesive before it dries; if the tile is too low, lift it up and add more adhesive. Finally, you may need to press down the tile with a suitable weight; consult the adhesive manufacturer's instructions.

Securing a loose tile. Lift the loose section of tile and spread a thin coat of adhesive on the underside with a narrow, flexible spatula. If only a corner of the tile is unstuck, carefully loosen more of it until you can turn the tile back far enough to spread the adhesive. Press the tile into place, making it level with surrounding tiles, and hold it down with a weight if this is specified by the adhesive manufacturer.

Patching Sheet Flooring

1 Cutting the patch. Tape a piece of replacement material over the damaged area, taking care to align it with the floor design. With a metal straightedge and a trimming knife, score the replacement material in the shape of the patch you want, following the lines in the design wherever possible. Using the scored outline as a guide, cut through both the replacement material and the floor covering beneath. Set aside the replacement material and gently chip through the adhesive on the underside of the damaged floor covering *(page 27)*. Remove the damaged covering and scrape off any adhesive on the subfloor.

2 Installing the patch. Spread adhesive over the exposed subfloor and set in the replacement patch as you would a tile *(page 27)*. Then hide the outline of the patch by covering its edge with heavy aluminium foil, dull side down, and pressing the foil several times with a very hot iron *(inset)*. This process, which can also be used to seal deep scratches in linoleum or solid vinyl, will partly melt the cut edges of the flooring so they form a solid and almost undetectable bond.

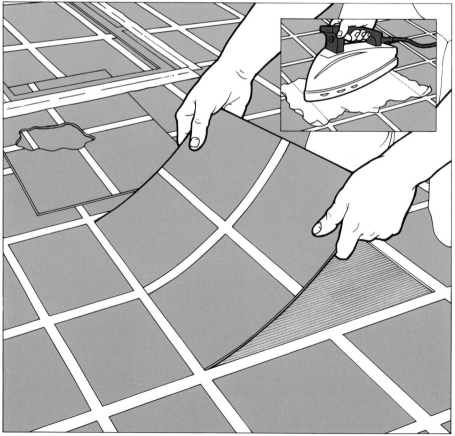

Flattening Bulges in Linoleum

Deflating a blister. Score, then slice, along the length of the blister with a trimming knife, extending the cut 12 mm beyond the blister at both ends. Try to cut along a line in the linoleum pattern to make the repair less conspicuous. With a spatula, spread a thin layer of adhesive through the slit on to the underside of the flooring. Press the linoleum down; if one edge overlaps because the flooring has stretched, use it as a guide to trim the edge beneath. Press the edges together and put a heavy weight on the repaired area for at least one hour.

Keeping That Resilient Beauty

Many people think a resilient floor needs a weekly scrubbing, then a coat of glossy polish. In fact, this is unnecessarily hard on the householder and not particularly good for the floor—too much washing can loosen the adhesive and polishing, too, is rarely necessary. Most modern resilient flooring has a permanent finish that is not only as hard, smooth and shiny as wax but is also tough enough to guard the floor against stains and dirt.

How often your floor should be cleaned depends on the material it is made of— some are more resistant to dirt than others *(page 46)*—and the traffic it bears. But the general rule of less is better is always applicable: do not polish when wet-mopping is sufficient; do not wet-mop when damp-mopping will do; do not damp-mop when a good sweeping is all that the floor requires.

Restraint with the scrubbing brush is particularly important when you are caring for a newly installed or recently repaired floor. Do not wash it for at least a week after the job is done, to give the adhesive time to form a solid bond. Then remove dirt with a damp mop or cloth and carefully scrape off spots of adhesive with a putty knife or fine steel wool.

For routine cleaning of resilient floors, a good daily sweeping plus an occasional damp-mopping is normally sufficient to remove dust and dirt. If you think your floor needs washing with detergent and water, avoid doing it more often than every three to six weeks.

However, even so-called permanent finishes eventually dull with age and wear. If you wish to restore a high-gloss finish to old flooring, rub in one or two light coats of a water-based floor polish.

The tough finishes that normally eliminate the need for polish also protect new resilient floors against stains from substances ranging from spilled food to splashed paint. Even so, you should quickly soak up any spillage and wash the affected area. If stains remain, they can usually be removed by a suitable cleaner. Bear in mind, however, that some of the chemicals you may use give off noxious fumes and can irritate skin, so work in a well-ventilated room and always wear rubber gloves. The following treatments are recommended for stains caused by common substances:

☐ Alcoholic drinks: rub the stained area with a cloth that has been dampened with surgical spirit.

☐ Blood: sponge with cold water; if that does not work, sponge with a solution of 1 part ammonia to 9 parts water.

☐ Candle wax, chewing gum and tar: cover with a plastic bag filled with ice cubes. When the material has become brittle, scrape off with a plastic spatula.

☐ Confectionery: rub with liquid detergent and fine steel wool, unless the floor is a "waxless" vinyl, in which case you should use a plastic scouring pad, warm water and powdered detergent.

☐ Cigarette burns: rub the burn with scouring powder and fine steel wool.

☐ Coffee: cover for several hours with a cloth saturated in a solution of 1 part glycerine (available at chemists) to 3 parts water. If the stain remains, rub it gently with scouring powder on a damp cloth.

☐ Fresh fruit: wearing rubber gloves, rub with a cloth dampened with a solution of 1 tablespoon oxalic acid, a powerful—and toxic—solvent available from chemists, and 600 ml water.

☐ Grease and oil: remove as much as possible with paper towels, then wash the stain with a cloth dampened in liquid detergent and warm water.

☐ Mustard or urine: cover for several hours with a cloth soaked in 3 to 5 per cent hydrogen peroxide (available at chemists) and cover that cloth with another soaked in household ammonia.

☐ Paint or varnish: rub with fine steel wool which has been dipped in warm water and liquid detergent.

☐ Leather and rubber scuff marks: scrub with a cloth soaked in a solution of 1 part ammonia to 9 parts water.

☐ Shoe or nail polish: rub with fine steel wool that has been soaked in warm water and scouring powder.

Some Easy Repairs for Hard-Surfaced Floors

The hard flooring materials—including marble, slate or ceramic tiles, and concrete or a mortar screed—are the most durable. They are also the most brittle and inflexible. All of them can be cracked by the fall of a heavy weight from above. If they are inadequately supported from below, they can be pulled apart by normal expansion and contraction in the supporting framework of a house. Under this invisible but constant stress, tiles will loosen and break. Concrete or mortar under similar stress will crack and crumble.

A tiled floor that is cracked throughout is usually a sign of trouble in the structure below. You may have to replace the entire floor by removing the old tiles, tightening up the subfloor (pages 8–10) and laying new tiles (pages 52–55). If only a few tiles are cracked, however, these can be simply replaced, one by one, using a cement-based adhesive. The techniques shown on these pages illustrate a professional's way of replacing an irregular tile at the base of a fixture or pipe on a ceramic tile floor; replacing marble or slate involves only slight variations in procedure.

After the tiles have been set and the adhesive has dried, the joints must be filled with grout—a decorative mortar which forms a barrier against dirt and moisture. Special waterproof grouts are available for kitchen and bathroom floors. Grouts come in a range of colours, so you can either match the existing one or replace all the grout with the new colour, giving a fresh look to an old tiled floor. Follow the manufacturer's instructions for mixing and applying the grout.

Like the flexible adhesives that simplify repairs to tiled floors, recently developed materials make it easy to patch concrete or a mortar screed. Cracks up to 3 mm wide can be filled with cement slurry (a mixture of cement and water), or with a proprietary patching compound; the latter can also be used to repair larger cracks. Where damage is extensive, the repair should be carried out with pre-mixed concrete.

At one time, even the most skilled craftsmen were not able to guarantee a large concrete patch. Dry concrete round the patch absorbed water from the new concrete, which stopped the new material from bonding with the old. The patch cracked because it could not cure without water. But a bonding agent such as polyvinyl acetate (PVA) or styrene butadiene rubber latex (SBR), applied to the edges of the old concrete just before the patch is made, prevents water loss and allows the pre-mixed concrete to remain flexible.

For an unfinished concrete slab, as shown on page 32, you will need to lay reinforcing mesh before pouring the pre-mixed concrete; a mortar screed can be patched in the same way, but as only the surface layer of damaged screed will need to be broken up, the reinforcing mesh will not, in this case, be required.

After patching a mortar screed, you can restore the appearance of the floor or, if you prefer, give it a completely new look with paint (page 33). Here, too, modern materials make a difference: new paints, specially formulated for this purpose and available in a variety of colours, resist blistering and peeling.

A Tight Fit Round a Fixture

1 Removing the grout. Wearing protective goggles, use a small cold chisel and hammer to chip out the grout at the edges of a damaged ceramic tile. Make a hole in each line of grout by striking the chisel straight down, then angle it to 45 degrees and chip outwards from the hole. Caution: tap the chisel lightly; heavy blows can cause cracks in the surrounding tiles. Use a wire brush or an old wood chisel to clean out any excess grout.

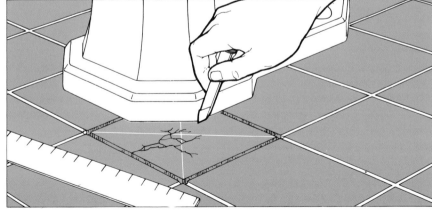

2 Removing the tile. On a ceramic tile, score from corner to corner, then along the base of the fixture, using a straightedge and tile cutter. Drill a hole through the centre of the tile with a 6 mm masonry bit. Hammer a cold chisel into the hole and, working towards the edges, break the tile into small pieces. Clean out the fragments of tile and scrape away the underlying adhesive with an old chisel. On a marble or slate tile, mark an X with a felt-tip pen and drill 18 mm holes 12 mm apart along the X, then along the base of the fixture, using a masonry bit. Break out the unwanted tile with a club hammer and cold chisel.

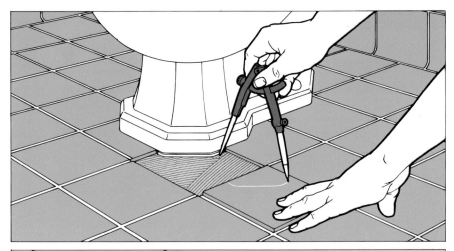

3 **Marking the new tile.** Set a new tile over the tile adjacent to the space you have cleared. Replace the pencil in a pair of compasses with a felt-tip pen and open the compasses to span the width of a single tile, then set the pen at the edge of the new tile and the point of the compasses at the corresponding point on the base of the fixture. Steady the tile with one hand and move the compasses slowly along the base of the fixture with the other until the pen has marked the shape of the base on the new tile.

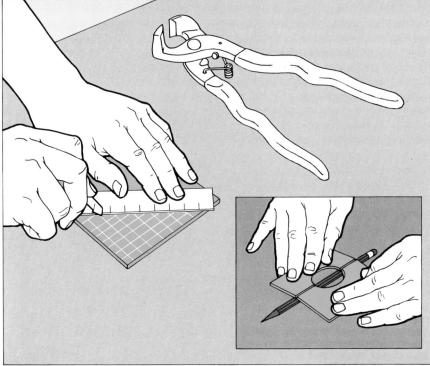

4 **Cutting the tile.** Using a tile cutter, score the line you have marked on the ceramic tile, then score a criss-cross pattern over the area to be cut away. Snip 3 mm pieces of tile away from the scored area with tile nippers. Angle the nippers so that you use only the corners of the blades; otherwise, the tile may break. Check the fit of the tile and smooth the edges with an emery cloth or carborundum stone. To cut a marble or slate tile, use a jigsaw fitted with a tungsten carbide blade, or a hacksaw fitted with a tungsten carbide rod saw.

A replacement for a tile round a pipe is easier to make. Measure the diameter of the pipe and drill a hole of the same size in the tile using a carbide-tipped hole saw. On marble or slate, mark the hole for the pipe on the tile, drill a starter hole at the centre and, using a coping saw fitted with a tungsten carbide blade, cut out the pipe hole. Score the tile from the pipe hole to the edges, using a tile cutter for ceramic tiles or an angle grinder for marble or slate tiles. Set the tile over a pencil on a flat surface and press down firmly on both sides until it breaks *(inset)*. Smooth the edges with an emery cloth.

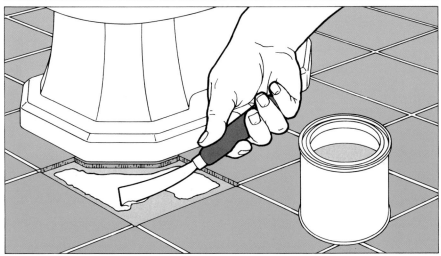

5 **Setting the tile in place.** Prime chipboard or plywood subfloors according to the adhesive manufacturer's instructions. Using a putty knife or plastic serrated spreader, apply adhesive to the exposed subfloor or mortar bed. If the new tile has indentations on its back, spread the adhesive over the back of the tile, but leave the border uncovered so that the adhesive does not ooze out when you press the tile in place. In either case, apply enough adhesive to raise the tile slightly higher than the ones round it. Use toothpicks or coins set on edge as spacers to keep the joints between ceramic tiles open and regular; marble and slate tiles normally butt tightly together. Set the new tile in position and press down firmly until it is level with the rest of the floor.

Let the adhesive set for 24 hours, remove the spacers and fill the joints with grout.

Durable Patches of Pre-Mixed Concrete

1 **Preparing a concrete floor.** Wearing gloves and goggles, use a sledgehammer or electric hammer drill *(page 56)* to break the damaged concrete into small, easily carried pieces. Clear away the rubble and use a cold chisel and hammer to slope the edges of the hole towards the centre. Roughen the edges with a wire brush and remove loose particles of concrete. Dig 100 mm below the bottom of the slab. Tamp the dirt inside the hole with the end of a 100 by 50 mm piece of timber and fill the hole as far as the bottom of the slab with clean 18 mm gravel.

2 **Cutting the reinforcing mesh.** Lay 100 by 100 by 4 mm gauge reinforcing wire over the hole and use metal shears to cut the wire to size; the ends of the wire should rest against the sloped edges of the concrete slab. Reinforcing wire comes in rolls or sheets; you can join two sections of wire by twisting the free strands together with pincers. Set two bricks under the wire to keep it centred between the top and bottom of the hole when the new concrete is poured.

3 **Pouring the patch.** Form a cone of pre-mixed patching concrete on a piece of hardboard, hollow out the top and pour water into the centre as the manufacturer specifies. Mix them together with a shovel until the concrete is firm but workable. Coat the edges of the hole with a PVA or SBR bonding agent, following the manufacturer's instructions. Before the coating dries, shovel the concrete into the hole, jabbing into it to force it against the sides of the hole and under the reinforcing wire. Fill the hole to the level of the slab, then add a few shovels of concrete to allow for settling and shrinking. With a rake, pull the wire about half way up to the surface of the concrete at all points, but be sure that none of the wire is exposed.

4 **Finishing the patch.** With a helper, sweep a straight 100 by 50 mm piece of timber across the surface of the patch to level it, working the board back and forth as you sweep. If you find depressions in the surface, fill them with concrete and go over the patch again with the piece of timber. A thin film of water will soon appear on the surface. When it evaporates and the surface sheen disappears, smooth the patch with a steel float *(page 30, Step 4)*. If the patch is too large to smooth from its edges, kneel on boards laid across it and work backwards from one side of the patch to the other, moving the boards as you go.

When the concrete hardens, sprinkle it with water and cover it with polythene to prevent moisture from escaping. Let the patch cure for three to seven days, checking it every day to be sure it is damp, and sprinkling it with water if this is necessary.

Cosmetics for a Screeded Concrete Floor

A concrete floor finished with a mortar screed has a certain rough beauty, but no one likes a stained floor and most people prefer one finished with a sealer or a paint. To remove stains or to paint, you must match materials and methods to your situation.

Most stains can be scrubbed away with water or a household detergent, but deep stains may require special treatment. Fold a piece of cheesecloth several times and lay it over the stained area. Then pour one of the chemicals listed below over the cloth. The chemicals will dis-solve the stain, and the cheesecloth will absorb the chemicals. Use the following recipes for specific stains:

☐ Rust: make a mixture of 1 part sodium citrate and 7 parts water.
☐ Copper or bronze: use 1 part ammonia to 9 parts water.
☐ Grease or oil: use a strong solution of household washing soda or a proprietary emulsifying agent obtainable from car accessory shops.
☐ Old paint: a suitable proprietary paint remover should be used.
☐ Mildew: use a proprietary fungicide.

Penetrating sealers are the simplest and least expensive finishes for concrete. They can be easily applied, dry in about eight hours and leave a thin film that protects against minor stains.

The paints listed below can be used on a clean, untreated mortar screed after a suitable waiting period. All of them can be spatter-dashed—a technique that obscures any small stains in concrete and creates a decorative effect *(left)*.

Epoxy or polyurethane coatings can be applied about a month after the mortar screed has been laid. They are relatively expensive but more durable than other types. Most come ready to apply, but a few manufacturers make "two-pack" coatings, for which the resins and hardeners must be pre-mixed. Epoxy and polyurethane paints usually need two coats; some need a primer. Most dry in six hours to a clear, tough, glossy finish.

Urethane alkyd paints are cheaper than epoxy and polyurethane paints, but not as hard-wearing. They need two or three coats and dry in about six hours.

Solvent-thinned, rubber-based paints are also not as long lasting as epoxy and polyurethane paints, but they are more water resistant; they are suitable for damp surfaces and humid areas. You will need three coats, the first applied two months after the mortar screed is laid. The paint dries in 30 minutes to four hours and the job can be done in a day.

Epoxy, polyurethane, urethane alkyd and rubber paints contain noxious solvents: work in a well-ventilated room.

Acrylic paints specially designed for finished concrete floors are cheaper than rubber, epoxy or polyurethane paints. Because they are water based, application and clean-up are easy, but they are far less durable than the others; do not use them on floors which are subject to continual traffic or where sudden drops in temperature are common. Apply three coats, beginning two months after the concrete is poured.

To spatter-dash a floor, apply two coats of paint. Before you apply the third and contrasting coat *(left)*, mask the walls with newspaper and put on goggles, gloves and a hat. Load a brush with the paint and then strike the handle, heel or bristles against the edge of a 50 by 25 mm board. Practise the technique over a sheet of paper before you begin.

2 New Floors: a Wealth of Choices

Tiling a floor. Square with the crossed strings in the centre of a floor, the first tile lies in position. These quarry tiles, durable and good-looking, would traditionally have been set in mortar, but a thin bed of modern adhesive over a screeded concrete surface is an alternative that has simplified the job of tiling.

A century or so ago the very rich walked on terrazzo or marble, but the most common flooring materials, at least in northern Europe, were timber floorboards or rough stones. Synthetics and modern industry changed all that. In 1863, a Briton named Frederick Walton invented a new kind of flooring—linoleum, made by mixing linseed oil, ground-up cork and natural resins. It was inexpensive, impervious to most spills and colourfully decorated with built-in patterns, and its popularity inspired the development of other man-made resilient floors of asphalt, rubber and plastic resins. Over the same period, mass production and modern transportation put floors of traditional materials that had been prohibitively expensive—wood parquet, ceramic tile, even marble—within the reach of millions of people.

Now, when installing a new floor, you can select the material best suited to the demands of a particular room. Durability and economy of upkeep can govern the choice for a workroom while appearance and comfort determine what will go underfoot in living room or bedroom. Wood, the traditional floor covering, is still the most versatile. Usually consisting of nailed strips or parquet blocks that are fastened down with adhesive, hardwood flooring is easy to walk on and is practical for most areas except the "wet rooms". Wood floors, while more expensive than resilient tiles or sheet flooring, last longer and provide a feeling of warmth that synthetic tiles lack. Wood strip and parquet floors also supply an extra layer of insulation. Hardwood floors are likely to shrink and swell with changes in moisture, but when the boards are installed in a reasonably dry area they will last as long as your home.

In kitchens and playrooms, the synthetic floorings that began with Frederick Walton's linoleum are the most popular. They are called resilient because they cushion the impact of feet or dropped objects. They come either as tiles that can be installed in a variety of designs *(pages 46–48)*, or in rolled sheets that can be cut to fit irregularly shaped rooms *(pages 50–51)*. In potentially damp areas, such as hallways or bathrooms, ceramic tiles, flagstones or other hard mineral surfaces surpass both wood and resilient materials in durability and water protection. Flagstones must be set in mortar. Ceramic tiles can be laid on either a level mortar screed or a chipboard subfloor by means of proprietary adhesives *(pages 52–53)*.

On a ground floor or in a basement, you can create a good floor by pouring one of concrete *(pages 56–61)*. Screeded concrete can serve as a base for finish flooring, can be left bare, or can be coated with paints for a heavy-duty surface that seals out grease and stains and will last for years with little more care than an occasional sweeping.

A Sound Base for a New Floor Covering

Any new floor covering requires a smooth, sound and stable base. If you are lucky, an existing floor surface of timber boards, resilient tiles or sheet material may need only local repairs *(pages 8–13 and 26–29)* before new flooring is laid on top. Often, however, you will have to install a completely new subfloor—because the existing surface is faulty, or because the new covering is not compatible with the old.

A timber floor that is too worn and uneven to provide a sound base for a new covering must be removed entirely and replaced with chipboard sheets *(below)* or with tongue and groove boards *(pages 40–41)*. Flooring-grade chipboard sheets are available in thicknesses of 18 mm, which is adequate for most rooms, and 22 mm, which should be used if joists are 450 mm or more apart; the most common sheet size is 2440 by 610 mm. For kitchens and bathrooms, you should use a specially treated, moisture-resistant chipboard.

Where you wish to floor over a concrete slab or screed, first use a moisture meter to check for damp. An alternative method of checking for damp is to lay a 450 mm square of heavy plastic over the concrete and seal the edges with tape. If drops of water condense on the plastic after a few days, you must lay a mortar screed over a damp-proof membrane *(pages 60–61)*.

Stone or ceramic tiles can be laid directly over a dry concrete floor that has been levelled with a screed or with a self-levelling compound. For reasons of both comfort and good adhesion, however, resilient or strip flooring is best laid on a chipboard subfloor installed on top of the concrete *(opposite page)*. Two layers of roofing felt or polythene serve to waterproof the concrete; the chipboard sheets are then secured to battens spaced across the floor to coincide with the sheet edges.

Laying a chipboard subfloor. Draw marks on the wall above the centre of each joist at both sides of the room. As you lay each chipboard sheet, use a straightedge and pencil to extend the joist lines across the sheet as a fixing guide. Leaving a 10 mm gap for expansion at the walls, lay the chipboard in a staggered pattern, with the shorter sides of each sheet parallel to the joists. Wherever possible, the joints between adjacent tongue and groove sheets should lie directly over a joist. Using 60 mm lost-head nails spaced at intervals of about 200 mm, secure the chipboard to the joists along the pencil lines. If you are working in an upstairs room, use 37 mm No. 8 countersunk screws to avoid the possibility of damage to the ceiling below. Where the ends of two sheets meet over a joist, stagger the nails or screws to prevent the joist from splitting. Punch all lost-head nails about 3 mm below the surface.

Once secured, tongue and groove sheets are difficult to lift, so make access panels over any pipes and cables that may need to be reached. Cut the panels so that two of the sides are supported by joist centres, and install noggings between the joists *(inset)* to support the other two sides.

Laying a Subfloor Over Concrete

1 Waterproofing the concrete. Cover the slab with lengths of lightweight roofing felt or 250 micron (1000 gauge) polythene, overlapping each length by about 100 mm and extending the ends up the wall face by the same amount—or, on an external wall, above the level of the damp-proof course. Place a second layer of overlapping strips cross-wise over the first *(right)*, again extending the ends up the wall face. The ends of both layers will later be covered by skirting boards.

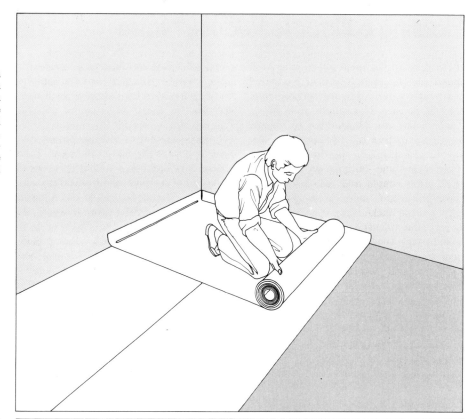

2 Installing battens. Lay 50 by 50 mm pre-treated timber battens across the room at 400 mm intervals, measured from centre to centre. Half way across the room, lay a length of 50 by 25 mm timber at right angles to the battens; temporarily secure this cross batten with 50 mm round-wire nails, leaving their heads protruding for easy removal. Starting from one side of the room parallel to the cross batten, lay sheets of tongue and groove chipboard across the battens in a staggered pattern *(opposite page)*. When you reach the centre of the room, remove the cross batten and finish laying the subfloor.

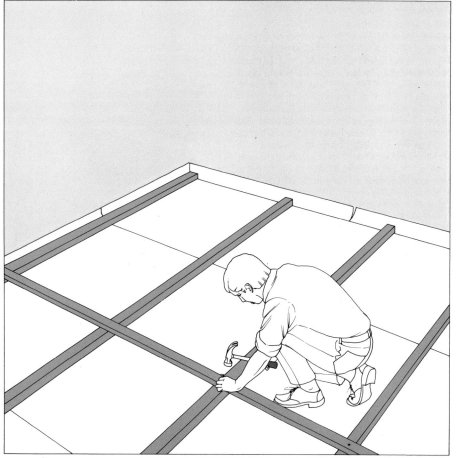

Floating a Floor to Reduce Noise

If footsteps in the room above your head sound like hammer blows, or a rocking chair rattles like a runaway steam train, then it is time to insulate your floors. These noises are transmitted by impact which means that the vibrations are carried by the structure—by the floorboards, nails, joists and ceilings—of the house itself. One simple and effective way of reducing impact noise is to put down carpets—the thicker they are, the better—or cork tiles at least 8 mm thick. But if you wish to enjoy the beauty of a plain wooden floor in an upstairs room or to put down vinyl or ceramic tiles, neither of which provide good sound insulation, it will be worth installing a floating floor.

The idea is to "float" the floor on a layer of insulation, thus isolating it from the rest of the house structure. Instead of putting a carpet on top of the floor, you are, in effect, putting one underneath it. The method described below for floating a floor over joists involves using a resilient quilt of 25 mm glass fibre insulation; rolls of mineral wool or sheets of expanded polystyrene can also be used for this purpose.

It is important that nothing connects the floating floor to the rest of the room. Take special care to provide insulation between the edges of the floor and the walls; make sure that skirting boards do not come in direct contact with the floor; above all, do not drive nails through chipboard or floorboards into the joists below—thus providing a bridge for sound. The battens that support the floor, and which must be thick enough to take a nail at least two and a half times the thickness of the flooring, are themselves floated on the insulation that covers the joists.

Where you are floating concrete on concrete *(opposite page, above)*, you need to separate the two surfaces with stiff insulating slabs of mineral fibre. To prevent the new screed from leaking down through the insulating layer and forming a bond with the old screed, you should cover the insulation material with a layer of polythene or tar-backed building paper.

Where you are floating chipboard or floorboards on concrete, first cover the concrete with glass fibre insulation, then install battens over the insulation *(page 37, Step 2)*. Alternatively, screw the battens to special acoustic clips which are mounted on rubber pads; no other insulating layer is then required.

Whatever type of floor you are floating, you can expect the level to rise by at least 50 mm. Trim the bottoms of inward-opening doors *(opposite page, below)* and install sloping thresholds of planed timber, isolated from the floating floor with a strip of cork, to meet the lower floor levels of adjoining rooms.

Laying a Soundproof Barrier

Insulating over joists. With the old floor and the skirting removed, lay strips of glass fibre insulation at right angles over the joists; lap the edges of the insulation up the wall to the height of the skirting you have removed. Some types of insulation are laid with the paper side up, and others with the paper side down, so read the manufacturer's instructions carefully. Directly over the joists, lay 50 by 37 mm battens on top of the insulation. Temporarily secure the battens with 50 mm round-wire nails, leaving their heads protruding. Do not nail the battens in the corner of the room where you plan to start laying the floor.

Cover the battens with either chipboard sheets *(page 36)* or tongue and groove boards *(pages 40–41)*, butting their edges against the insulation that laps up the walls. Remove the temporary fixing nails from the battens as you work across the room. When the new floor is installed, replace the skirting boards over the turned-up edges of the insulation, leaving a 5 mm gap between the boards and the floor. A thin cork strip inserted into this gap will ensure that the floating floor is completely isolated from the rest of the room.

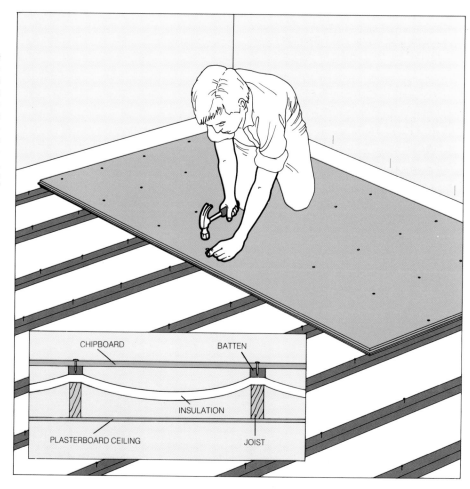

CHIPBOARD   BATTEN

INSULATION

PLASTERBOARD CEILING   JOIST

Insulating over concrete. Remove the finish floor and the skirting, then place vertical strips of 100 by 25 mm glass fibre insulation along the base of each wall. Cover the concrete with insulating slabs of mineral fibre *(right)*, butting their edges against the insulation at the walls. Cover the slabs with a layer of 1000 gauge 25 micron polythene, lapping the sheet edges up the walls to the height of the old skirting and overlapping adjoining sheets by 150 mm. Spread the sheeting so that it lies flat and tuck it carefully into the corners. Mix and lay a screed at least 35 mm thick over the polythene *(pages 60–61)*. When this has thoroughly cured, re-lay the finish floor and replace the skirting.

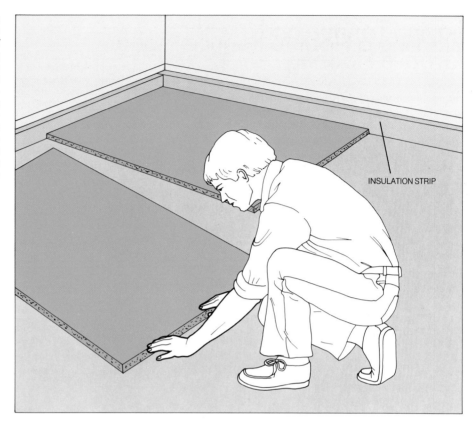

INSULATION STRIP

Trimming for a New Floor

Shortening doors that open inwards. Measure from the top of the door lining to the new surface of your floor. Transfer this measurement from the top to the bottom of inward-opening doors, reducing the distance by a few millimetres to allow for clearance over the floor, then square a line across the face of the door. Using a straight piece of timber as a guide, saw along the cutting line to cut off the bottom edge of the door. Finally, mark and cut off the bottoms of any architraves.

Laying Tongue and Groove Flooring

A tongue and groove timber floor is simple to install, yet can be both hard-wearing and elegant. Softwood boards—usually of European redwood or whitewood—can serve either as a subfloor to be covered with carpet or resilient flooring, or, protected by tough, modern sealants, as an attractive finish floor. Hardwood strips, although considerably more expensive, provide a durable finish floor that will withstand continual wear and tear.

In the demonstration on the right, softwood boards are nailed directly into joists; hardwood boards can also be laid over joists, but narrow strips are best laid over an existing timber floor as shown on pages 42–44. In both cases, slight gaps between the boards and walls that are bowed or out of square can be covered with skirting boards or with quadrant moulding, but for larger gaps you may have to cut the final board at an angle.

The tongue and groove joints are locked tightly together with the help of folding wedges and a "dog", a U-shaped metal spike that is driven into joists or a timber subfloor with a hammer. Blocks of scrap wood nailed to the joists may be used instead of dogs; to speed the job, you can hire a special tool known as a flooring cramp.

Both softwood boards and hardwood strips are available in a range of widths, and in lengths varying from 1 metre to 5 metres or more. They are sold by the square metre; when ordering, you should allow at least 10 per cent for wastage. Use softwood boards 18 mm thick for laying over joists at 400 mm centres, and 21 mm thick if the joists are more widely spaced. Hardwood boards wider than 200 mm must be fixed with screws in order to prevent buckling (*page 45*).

Floorboards are susceptible to warping and swelling caused by moisture. If your house is centrally heated, choose timber with a low moisture content (about 10 per cent). If you have underfloor heating, or if you plan to lay a timber floor in a kitchen or bathroom, seek the advice of your supplier. All timber should be left for a week or so to adjust to the temperature and humidity of the environment before it is laid.

1 **Nailing the first board.** Select a board long enough to span the room at right angles to the joists with a few millimetres' clearance at each end. Look along the edges to make sure it is straight. Then, working on a chipboard platform, align the tongued edge of the board 10 mm from one wall—this gap will allow for any expansion of the flooring after it has been installed. Secure the board at each joist with a cut floor brad or lost-head nail, two and a half times the thickness of the board in length, driven in near the tongued edge.

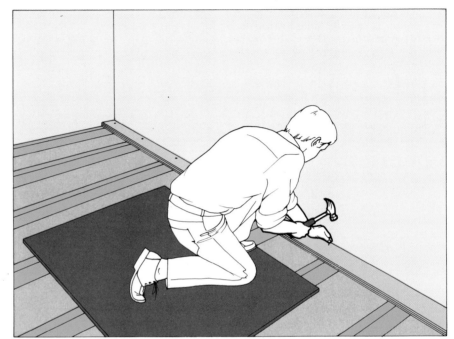

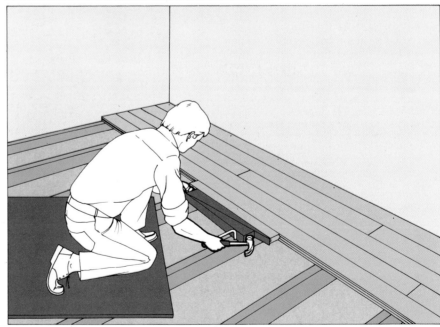

2 **Locking tongues into grooves.** Lay four complete rows of boards, loosely slotting tongues into grooves and using one long board for the last row. Butt short boards together over the joists—cut them to fit if necessary—and stagger the joints in adjoining rows. At every fourth joist across the room, slot a tongued offcut into the grooved edge of the board, then hammer a dog into the joist at right angles to and about 75 mm away from the offcut. Insert folding wedges between the dog and the offcut. Using two hammers, knock together the wedges (*above*) to force the tongues of the floorboards tightly into their corresponding grooves.

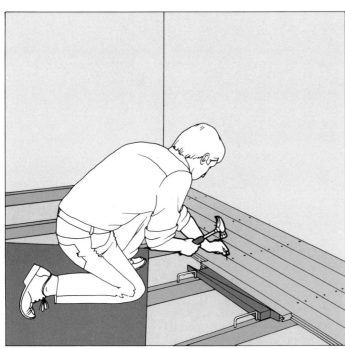

3 **Face-nailing the boards.** Fasten the grooved edge of the first board with a brad or lost-head nail driver through to each joist. Then fasten the next three boards with two fixings in each joist. Where there is more than one board in a row, fasten the first board then use a crowbar to force the next one against it before completing the fixing—this will ensure a tight joint between board ends. For the last row, use only one fixing per joist, driven through the tongued edge: leave the grooved edge free until you have laid another four rows of boards and locked them together. Remove the dogs and folding wedges, then work across the rest of the room, locking and fixing the boards in the same way.

4 **Cutting a board to fit.** When there is no longer enough room to use folding wedges, lay the last two or three rows of full-width boards. Then, with a circular saw or handsaw, cut a tongued strip of board to fit the remaining gap, allowing 10 mm clearance between its cut edge and the wall.

5 **Completing the floor.** Lay the tongued strip in place, then, to hold the boards steady for nailing, drive wooden wedges between the strip and the wall, forcing the last rows of boards together. Fix the boards to the joists and remove the wedges. Finally, replace the skirting boards.

Laying Hardwood Strips

1 **Fixing the first row.** Position a long, straight strip 10 mm from a skirting board and at right angles to the existing floorboards, with its grooved edge towards the wall. To secure the grooved edge of the strip, drill nail holes at 400 mm intervals as close as possible to the edge, then drive in 37 mm lost-head nails or cut floor brads. Secret-nail the tongued edge with 37 mm lost-head nails or brads driven in at 400 mm intervals through the base of the tongue *(page 13, Step 5)*. Punch this second row of fixings about 3 mm below the surface with a nail punch. If the first board does not span the room, secure additional boards to complete the first row.

2 **Staggering the strips.** Working out from the first row, loosely position seven or eight rows of strips in a staggered pattern, with end joints in adjoining rows at least 150 mm apart. Then, moving the strips back as necessary to give yourself room for working, use a grooved offcut, folding wedges and a dog *(page 40, Step 2)* at intervals of about 600 mm to lock the first and second rows together. Secret-nail the second row through its tongued edge and punch the nail heads. Work across the rest of the room in the same way, paying careful attention to the pattern of the joints. At the finishing side of the room, insert grooved lengths between the last full-width row and the skirting as described on page 41, Step 5.

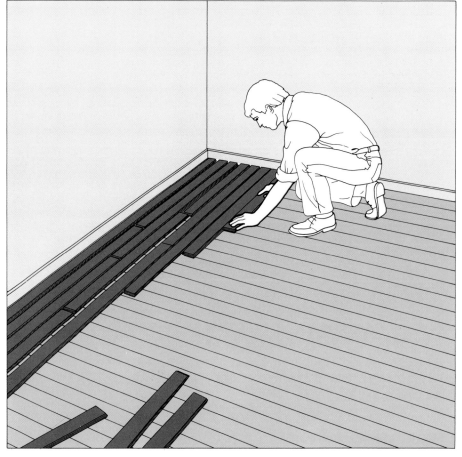

3 Framing special borders. Using a mitre box, saw boards at 45-degree angles to frame the hearth of a fireplace *(inset)*. Cut off the boards' tongues where necessary to make them fit flush with adjoining boards. Face-nail them into place.

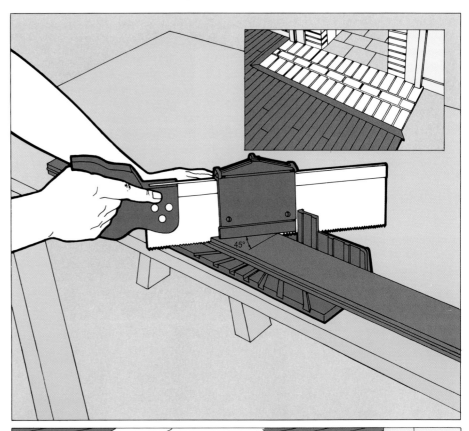

4 Reversing tongue direction. To install hardwood strips in a hall or cupboard that opens on to the grooved side of the starting row, join groove to groove with a strip of plywood cut to the width of two tongues. Insert the plywood strip into the groove of the starting row, lock the loose board in position with a dog and folding wedges and then secret-nail through its tongue.

5 **Finishing off a doorway.** With a saw and a smoothing plane, remove the tongued face of a hardwood strip, then bevel the face to make a smooth transition at a doorway where the new floor meets a lower floor. Face-nail the bevelled strip 50 mm from each end and at 300 mm intervals with 37 mm lost-head nails along the grooved edge and 32 mm panel pins along the bevelled edge *(right)*. Punch nails about 3 mm below the surface. For a doorway at right angles to the new flooring, remove both tongued and grooved edges from a hardwood strip, bevel one edge and secure as described above; this strip is best secured before the flooring is laid, to provide a straight edge against which the ends of the flooring strips can be butted.

6 **Laying expansion strips.** Wedge cork strips into the 10 mm gap between the long edges of the flooring strips and the skirting. The cork acts as a cushion that contracts or expands with the swelling or shrinking of the timber.

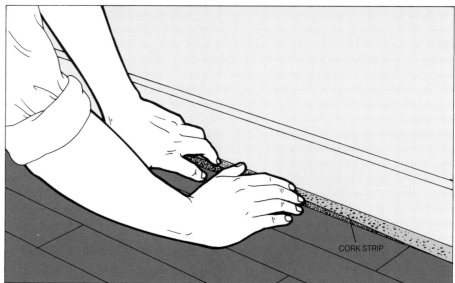

CORK STRIP

7 **Installing quadrant moulding.** Fix 19 mm quadrant moulding round the perimeter of the room, using 32 mm panel pins driven in at 200 mm intervals. Drive the pins horizontally through the middle of the moulding into the skirting; this will allow the new floor to shrink or expand without damaging the moulding.

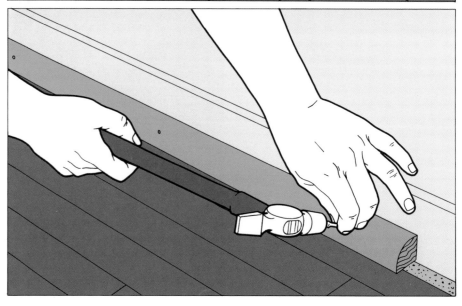

Screws to Hold Wide Hardwood Boards

1 Drilling the pilot holes. Use a 12 mm spade bit to drill partly through the ends of the boards. A piece of masking tape stuck on the bit 6 mm from the squared end of the cutting edge will serve as a guide for the depth of the hole. Stagger additional screw holes at 500 mm intervals along the faces of long boards.

2 Securing the boards. Drive 37 mm No. 8 countersunk screws into the pilot holes and through the boards. Then cover the screw heads with pellets 6 mm deep and 12 mm in diameter, cut from a hardwood offcut with a pellet cutter fitted to an electric drill. Secure the pellets with PVA adhesive, making sure that the grain of the pellets runs in the same direction as the grain of the floor. Plane off the tops of the pellets flush with the surface of the boards.

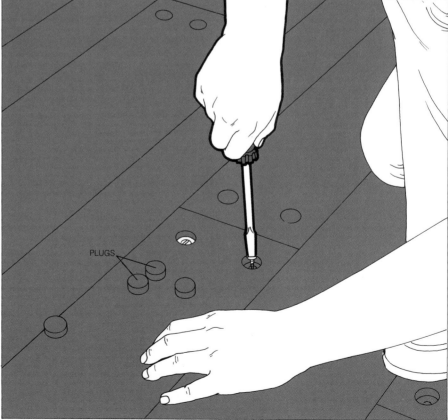

PLUGS

Eye-Catching Patterns in Sheet and Tile

Resilient flooring, sturdy and easy to care for, comes in both sheets *(pages 50–51)* and tiles. The tiles lend themselves to imaginative design and are available in a range of materials *(below)*. Most tiles are 300 mm square, though there are also 229 and 250 mm versions. Wood tiles *(page 49)*, often called parquet, are installed in much the same way as resilient tiles, and also can provide variations in pattern. Choose tiles according to the amount of traffic they will bear and the floor design you have in mind.

You can lay a tile floor all in one colour, of course, but once you know how to design a floor you can use tiles to hide visual defects—stripes running across the width make a room look broader, for example—to highlight particular areas of the room, or to decorate your floor with any pattern that strikes your fancy.

Begin by measuring your room and calculating the number of tiles you will need; then draw the floor on graph paper *(opposite page, top)* and work out the design you want by filling in the squares with the appropriate tile colours.

Resilient tiles must be laid on a sound, level surface such as a chipboard subfloor *(pages 36–37)*. Timber boards, which shift too much to provide a firm base, or a mortar screed should be covered with a hardboard or plywood underlay—a thickness of about 6 mm should be suitable for most surfaces. Prepare hardboard by painting the rough side with water and allow it to dry out partially for 48 hours. This treatment will prevent subsequent problems with shrinkage. Secure ply or hardboard, with its rough side uppermost, to the floor with ring-shanked annular nails 9 mm in from the edges and 100 mm apart.

Before laying tiles on screeded concrete, check for moisture and cure any dampness *(page 36)*. If the concrete is dry, repair any cracks or holes *(pages 30–33)*, flatten bumps with an abrasive block and fill in depressions with a self-levelling compound. Then coat the floor surface with a clear waterproofing solution and allow it to dry before laying tiles.

You can lay a new resilient tile floor over an old one if you remove wax and other finishes and repair indentations, holes or loose tiles *(pages 26–29)*.

After you have worked out your design and prepared the floor, set up guidelines by the method shown *(opposite page, centre)*. Tiles are laid either on the square, with their edges parallel to the walls, or on the diagonal, with their edges at a 45-degree angle to the walls: the guidelines you make will ensure that the tiles are correctly aligned in either direction. Test your plot by making a dry run of tiles *(opposite page, bottom)*. This will enable you to adjust your borders and thus avoid the tedious business of cutting tiny pieces of tile to fit along a wall. If you are trying a complex design, you may want to do a dry run over the entire floor.

Once you have tested your design with a dry run, laying the floor is largely a matter of sticking down the tiles. Some come ready glued, but most require an adhesive *(page 26–27)*; follow the manufacturer's instructions. In the case of parquet flooring, a more viscous adhesive may be recommended. Both latex-based and solvent-based adhesives work best when the room is warmer than 21°C. Bear in mind, however, that solvent-based adhesives are inflammable, so if you are using this type make sure the room is well ventilated and extinguish any pilot lights or other flames.

Selecting the Right Resilient Flooring

Material	Form	Advantages	Limitations
Cork	Tile	Most resilient flooring; deadens sound	Wears rapidly; poor resistance to heavy loads; stains badly unless coated with vinyl
Linoleum	Sheet, tile	Inexpensive; durable; easily cleaned; good grease resistance	Damaged by moisture; requires waxing; limited availability
Rubber	Tile	Very resilient; resists dents; quiet; waterproof	Slippery when wet; poor resistance to grease; requires frequent polishing to maintain gloss
Vinyl	Sheet, tile	Outstanding durability; fine resistance to stains, dents; deadens sound; easy maintenance; variety of colours and patterns	Relatively expensive; poor resistance to burns
Vinyl-asbestos	Tile	Durable; stain-resistant; inexpensive; widely available	Not as resilient or quiet as vinyl

Creating the Design

Planning on paper. On graph paper, plot a design for a floor laid on the square *(near right)* or on the diagonal *(far right)*, letting each block represent one tile. To find out how many tiles to plot to a side, divide the dimensions of the room by the size of the tile. For example, if you use 300 mm tiles, the 6 metre square design *(near right)* requires 20 per side. If 229 mm tiles are used, it requires 26.2 per side, but plot it for 27; always count fractions of tiles as whole tiles.

To work out the total number of tiles required, divide the length and width of your room by the size of the tile and multiply the two results. If tiles of two colours are to be laid, count the squares of one colour and subtract from the total to see how many tiles you need of each; add 5 per cent for waste and repairs.

Guidelines for the dry run. Divide the room into equal quadrants with two chalk lines stretched between nails set at the midpoints of both pairs of facing walls. Make sure the strings intersect at 90-degree angles by measuring from the intersection 900 mm on one string and 1200 mm on the other. The diagonal between these points should measure 1500 mm. Do not snap the chalk lines.

If your pattern is to be laid on the diagonal, measure the shorter guideline from the intersection to the wall, then set nails into the wall at points that distance to either side of the guideline nail. Repeat this on the opposite wall and stretch chalked strings diagonally between the nails *(inset)* so that they bisect the angles formed by the original guidelines.

Making a dry run. For a pattern laid on the square, lay dry tiles in one quadrant, starting from the intersection and duplicating the colours plotted on your graph paper. If the dry run ends more than half a tile from the wall, snap both chalk lines and remove them. If the last tiles are less than half a tile's width from the wall, move the rows to make larger gaps so you will not have to cut and lay small pieces. Set the chalk lines in the new place and snap them.

To check a diagonal pattern, lay dry tiles point to point along the perpendicular lines defining one quadrant and lay an extra row along the diagonal guideline *(inset)*. When laying a chequerboard pattern, you will achieve the best effect if the floor ends at each wall in a saw-tooth line of half tiles. Add a border of tiles set on the square wide enough to make the diagonally laid field end in a saw-tooth; if differences in the widths of borders on two adjacent walls are disturbing, make the borders at least two tiles wide.

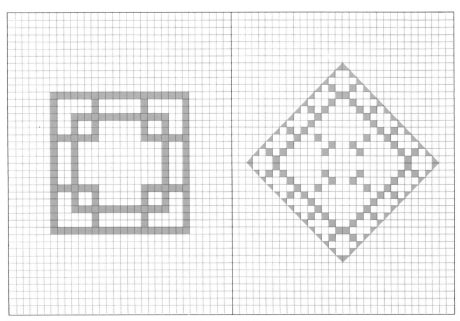

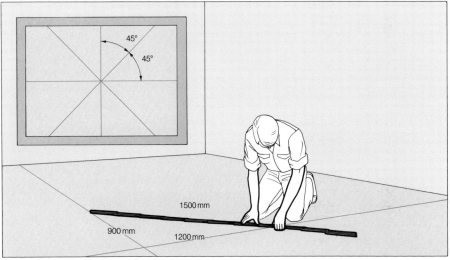

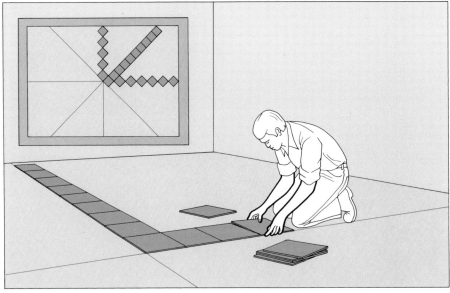

Setting the Tiles

Laying tiles and adhesive. With a notched trowel held at a 45-degree angle to the floor, spread adhesive along one chalk line—if you are laying tiles in an on-the-square pattern—working from the intersection towards a wall. Leave parts of the line uncovered for guidance, and make your layer about half the thickness of a tile. Set this row of tiles, butting each tile against one already laid and dropping it into place. Do not slide a tile: that will force adhesive on to its surface. Set a second row of tiles along the perpendicular chalk line, then fill the area between the rows in a pyramid pattern in such a way that each new tile butts against two already laid *(top inset)*. When you finish a section, roll it with a hired 18kg linoleum roller or a rolling pin on which you put most of your weight. To lay a diagonal pattern *(bottom inset)*, set tiles point to point over the perpendicular chalk line. Lay another row of tiles with their sides along the diagonal chalk line. Then fill in the area between rows, working from the intersection towards the wall.

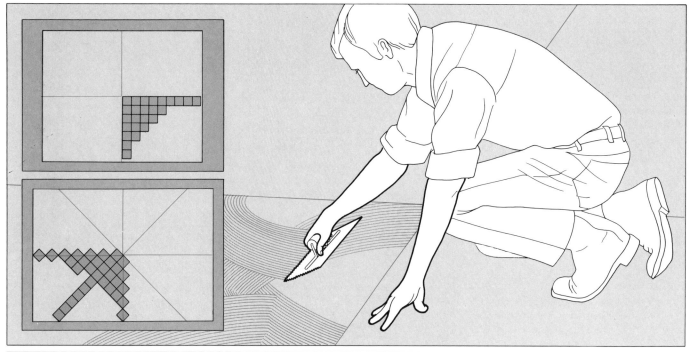

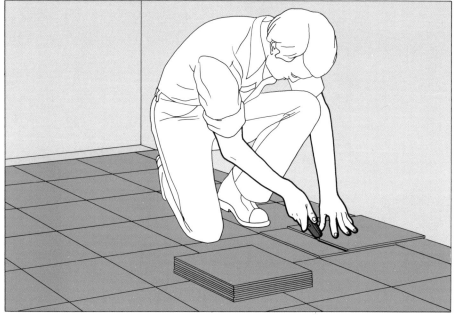

Trimming a border tile. Place two loose tiles squarely on top of the last whole tile in a row and slide the upper one across the untiled gap until it touches a wall; then, using the edge of the top tile as a guide, score the one beneath with a trimming knife. Snap the tile along the scored line. The piece that was not covered by the guide tile will fit into the border, with its snapped edge against the wall. Cut oddly shaped tiles—those around door mouldings, for example—by the methods shown on pages 30–31.

If your floor is diagonally laid, score tiles from corner to corner, using a straightedge, and snap them to make triangular half tiles to fill the saw-tooth edge of the diagonal pattern. If you also have a square-set border, trim tiles for it as described above.

Patterns for Parquetry

Parquet panels and tiles come in a number of sizes and shapes with which you can lay a handsome floor. Panels comprise strips of wood attached to a flexible backing, sometimes arranged in a basketweave pattern; square or rectangular tiles can be laid in a variety of patterns such as those shown on the right. The design and installation techniques are much like those for resilient tiles *(pages 46–48)*; when plotting your design, however, you may need to use more than one square of the graph paper to represent each tile, and you should indicate the direction of the wood grain. In elongated tiles, the grain runs lengthways.

While resilient tile floors have a border of trimmed tiles on four sides, wooden floors should have a border of whole tiles on the sides of the room where there are doorways; this is because the glue under a full-sized wooden tile provides a stronger bond in heavy traffic areas. Guidelines are set up just as they are for resilient tiles *(page 47)*, but when you make a dry run you may need to adjust the lines to get a full-tile border on a door side.

Wooden tiles absorb moisture, so let them stand for 72 hours in the room where they will be laid—this will get them used to the humidity. Also, leave a 10 mm space between the border tiles and the walls to allow for the tiles' expansion. Insert a thin strip of 10 mm cork, available at your flooring retailer, in the space.

When laying the tiles, pay special attention to the grain patterns which you have marked on your plot. Use an adhesive recommended by the manufacturer (this will usually be bitumen based). Tiles with tongue and groove edges may require no adhesive at all, as their interlocking sides will secure them adequately.

Laying the "herringbone" pattern. Lay the first rectangular tile along a diagonal guideline, one corner set in the intersection. Lay the second tile at the end of and perpendicular to the first, and the third tile at the end of and perpendicular to the second, as shown on the right. Use the chalk lines and these three tiles as guidelines for laying the next three and continue until you reach the wall. Repeat in the other sections of the room until you have completed the floor *(inset)*.

Setting parquet tiles in place. Making sure that the grain pattern duplicates the one on your graph paper, butt a parquet tile tightly against the edges of adjacent tiles. Tap the tile with a mallet cushioned by a wooden block. The tiles should be laid in the pyramidal manner used for resilient tiles *(opposite page, above)*. Measure border tiles as you would resilient tiles *(opposite page, below)*, but mark them with a pencil instead of scoring them, and cut them with a fine-toothed handsaw.

Laying the "Haddon Hall" pattern. Starting at the intersection of your guidelines, lay a square of four rectangular tiles bordering one square tile *(below)*. The first two rectangular tiles should be laid perpendicular to each other along the guidelines. Lay the floor pyramidally from this block until it is complete *(inset)*.

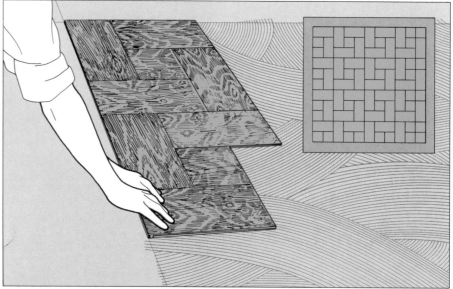

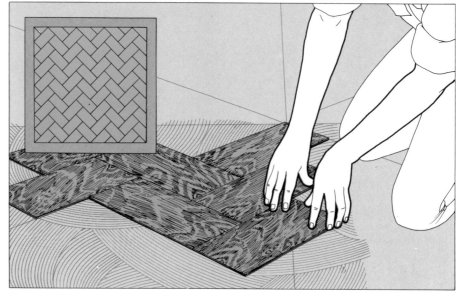

49

Template for a Cut-to-Fit Floor

Sheet vinyl provides the springiness and pattern variety of resilient tiles in an essentially seamless surface—moistureproof and dirt-resisting. In large rooms, vinyl is unrolled, trimmed to fit and fastened in place with adhesive. In small areas like the one shown on these pages, a floor pattern cut from felt paper can speed the job. The pattern is laid on the sheet vinyl and the flooring is cut to fit.

Guidelines can be made on the paper and the sheet vinyl with a pair of compasses or a tool called a scriber, available at hardware shops. The scriber resembles a pair of compasses fitted with a second sharp point in place of the pencil, and has a knurled nut that locks the points at any spacing you choose. To mark very resilient sheet vinyls, on which scratches may not show, replace one of the scriber points with a felt-tip pen.

Begin the job by rough-cutting the felt paper to lie flat in the room. Then run one point of the scriber round the walls; the other point will scratch the outline of the room and all its interruptions on to the paper. Lay the vinyl in another room, flat if possible, for at least 24 hours to adjust to room temperature. Then spread the pattern over the vinyl and reverse the scribing procedure by running one point along the scratches on the felt paper; the other will mark the room's outline on the vinyl. Cut the vinyl out and lay it into the room.

Fold the sheet half way back on itself and, using a notched trowel, coat the floor with a non-inflammable water-based acrylic adhesive; use a type recommended for the material being applied *(page 26)*. Roll the vinyl over the adhesive and repeat the procedure. In small areas it may be possible to stick down the edges simply with double-sided tape.

Because sheet vinyl comes in widths of up to 4 metres, you may be able to avoid seams except for the short ones necessary to fit the vinyl round obstacles. At such places, slit the vinyl from its nearest edge, then make a cutout for the pipe or post. When you lay the flooring, repair the slits with a seam-sealing fluid, available from flooring retailers, which makes the joint almost invisible.

1 **Fitting the felt paper.** Unroll the felt paper along the longest side of the room, slicing with a trimming knife about 25 mm from the walls, stairs, door architraves and all permanent obstructions. Fasten one end of the strip to the floor with drawing pins across its width. Then crawl from that end of the room to the other, running your hands over the paper ahead of you to stroke it smooth; insert drawing pins at about 600 mm intervals to hold the paper flat. Lay, trim and pin enough sheets to cover the room, overlapping them about 150 mm.

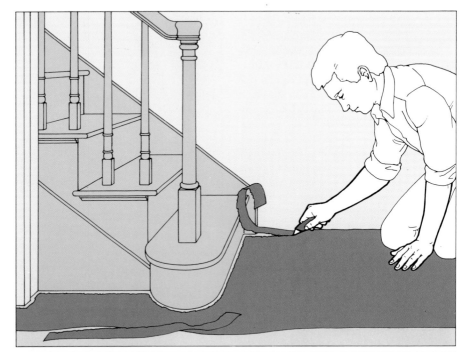

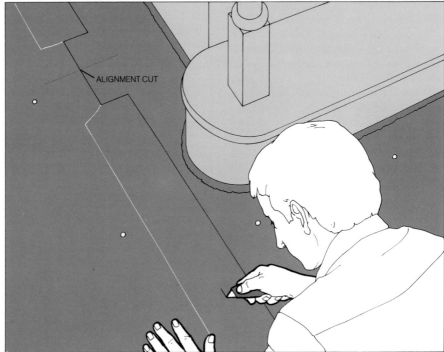

ALIGNMENT CUT

2 **Cutting notches to align the sheets.** Every 600 mm along an overlap between sheets, make a 200 mm alignment cut through both sheets with a trimming knife. Make additional cuts from the ends of the alignment cut to the edge of the top sheet and discard the rectangular scrap you have cut out. Reach under the notch and cut or tear away a similar notch along the edge of the bottom sheet. The sheets will butt along the alignment cut; the other cuts or tears are not critical. Chalk a short line across the alignment cut, marking both sheets.

3 **Scribing the pattern.** Set the points of a scriber about 50 mm apart and, keeping an imaginary line between the points perpendicular to the walls, architraves or stair risers, pull one point round the edge of the room, letting it ride along the walls; the other point will scratch a line on the paper. The span between the points must not change during the job; to check the setting, scribe part of a circle on to the felt paper *(inset)*, then periodically set the points at the centre and rim of the circle.

Remove the drawing pins and carry the paper to the room where you have unrolled the vinyl.

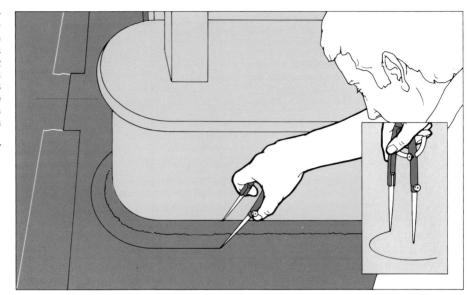

4 **Positioning the pattern.** Lay the sheets of paper on the vinyl, butting top and bottom sheets at each alignment notch and lining up the chalk marks across them. Slide the pattern over the vinyl so that any pattern in the vinyl will line up along the longest wall, using the scriber to check the final position. (Remember that you will cut the vinyl as far outside the scribed lines as the distance between the scriber points.) Pin the pattern to the vinyl—the pinholes will not show after the vinyl is laid.

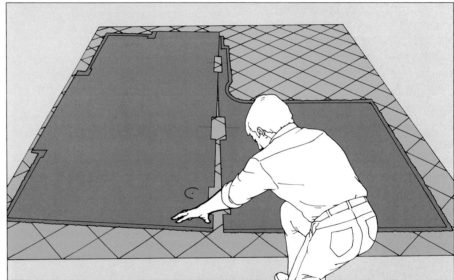

5 **Cutting the vinyl.** Holding the scriber exactly as you did in Step 3, trace the scribed line on the paper with one scriber point; the other point will scratch a cutting line on the surface of the vinyl. If a scratched line does not show up on the vinyl, replace one point of the scriber with a felt-tip pen, using the partial circle on the felt paper to check the setting. Cut through the flooring along the cutting line with a trimming knife; the common straight blade will serve, but many professionals prefer to use a hooked blade (these are available at hardware shops).

Lay the vinyl into position in the room. Fold one side half way back and spread adhesive on to the floor *(page 48)*. Set the vinyl back into position and roll out any air bubbles with a heavy roller, hired from your flooring retailer, or with a rolling pin. Fold back the other side, spread adhesive and roll out. Finally secure edging strips over exposed vinyl edges, as in doorways.

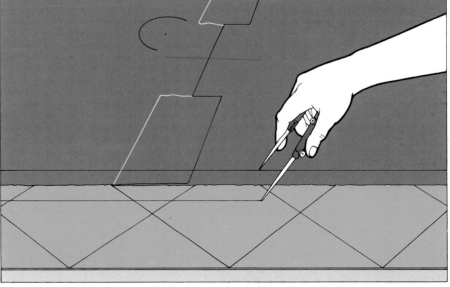

Laying Stone and Ceramic Tiles in Mortar

For many floors, the advantages of hard mineral materials may well outweigh the desirability of resilience provided by wood or vinyl. Halls, hearths, kitchens and bathrooms can all benefit from the beauty and durability of ceramic or stone tiles.

Ceramic tile retailers, supplied by artisans abroad as well as by a big domestic industry, offer a dazzling variety of sizes, finishes and colours, from unglazed, earth-coloured quarry tiles 150 mm square and 12 mm thick to glazed and patterned tiles up to 300 mm square. Mosaic tiles consist of small ceramic squares or shapes held together by sheets of adhesive paper or hessian. Whatever tile you choose, remember that grooved, ribbed or studded surfaces will help reduce slipperiness.

Slate and various kinds of sandstone, limestone and quartzite, all available in tile-shaped rectangles of uniform thickness, also make attractive, impermeable floors and can be laid in the same way as ceramic tiles. Marble, the grandest of all floor coverings, comes in a variety of sizes, 300 mm square by 10 mm thick being among the most popular. Despite its density, marble absorbs liquids and should be protected with transparent silicone sealer. The poultices used for cleaning concrete

(page 33) will get rid of most stains.

Ceramic, stone or other hard-mineral tiles are best laid over a screeded concrete floor, but they can also be put down on an existing hard-tile or vinyl surface, provided that it is clean, sound and level. If you wish to lay hard tiles over timber boards, you must first cover the boards with an underlay of 12 mm exterior-grade plywood or of 18 mm moisture-resistant chipboard screwed at 225 mm centres. Prime this subfloor with a sealant recommended for use with your adhesive at least 24 hours before laying the tiles.

Check a concrete floor for dampness *(page 36)* and, if necessary, install a moisture barrier and a new screed *(pages 56–61)*. If the concrete is dry but uneven, follow the method for levelling the surface described on page 46.

Before you begin to prepare a floor for laying hard tiles, remove skirting boards and any inward-opening doors. The tiles which you lay will raise the finished floor level by at least 12 mm, so you need to trim down the bottom edges of any doors which will open over the floor to ensure adequate clearance *(pages 38–39)*.

Lay out the tiles, using the method shown on page 47, but in place of chalk

lines stretch mason's string tautly between masonry pins driven into the walls 18 mm from the floor. Bear in mind any directional pattern, such as the grain of marble, when designing your floor.

Hard tiles are traditionally bedded in mortar, a technique still used for irregular shaped tiles such as flagstones *(page 55)*, but factory-made tiles and modern adhesives have simplified this process. Tile adhesive is available ready mixed or as a cement-based powder that you mix with water. Your tile dealer will recommend a suitable brand. Apply it with a rectangular "box-notch" trowel, as shown here, or use a spreader of the kind specified by the manufacturer. Cover no more than 1 square metre at a time.

Finish the job by replacing doors and skirting boards. For a formal look or for protection against splashes in bathrooms, buy ready-made matching trim from your tile retailer. For stone floors, you can make your own base trim by cutting 300 by 300 mm tiles into 100 by 300 mm strips. Smooth and bevel or round rough edges with silicon carbide sanding discs in an electric drill, using grits 80, 150 and 320 in succession. Secure trim to the wall with water-resistant organic adhesive.

1 **Applying the adhesive.** Beginning in one of the corners where the reference strings cross, use a box-notch trowel to spread a layer of adhesive. Then hold the trowel nearly vertical and drag the teeth on the subfloor, leaving a row of ridges.

2 **Laying the first tile.** Place a tile on the adhesive with one corner at the crossed strings. Twist it slightly several times as you press down firmly; use full pressure on big tiles. With the handle of a mason's trowel, tap the edges of the tile until it lines up exactly with the strings. Check with a spirit level along both dimensions and diagonally; tap down any high sides of the tile. Pick up excess adhesive for re-use.

It is wise to check your first tile by lifting it off the adhesive and finding out if it made full contact; if it did not, then make a new bed with more adhesive and re-lay the tile with more twisting and pressure. If you are using quarry tiles that have deeply scored undersides, trowel adhesive into the scores before setting.

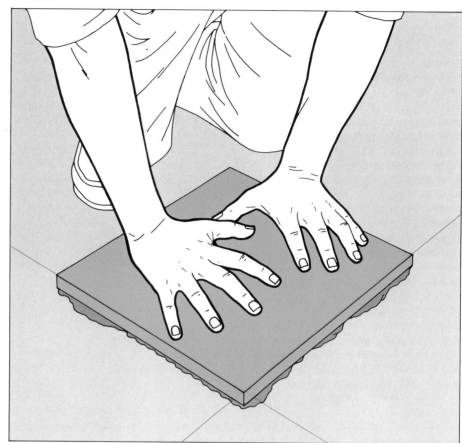

3 **Filling in the field.** Lay tiles, aligned with strings, in all four directions from the first; when the cross thus formed has set, remove the strings and fill in the quarters. Unless the tiles have self-spacing lugs cast on their bottom edges, use rounded toothpicks or ready-made spacer pegs to hold them 3 mm apart. Since tiles may not be cut to exact size, measure frequently from the centre lines and adjust spacing to keep joints squared. Use a spirit level on a straight length of timber to check and adjust the height of the tiles against the central tile as you set them. At obstacles, use the techniques shown on pages 30–31.

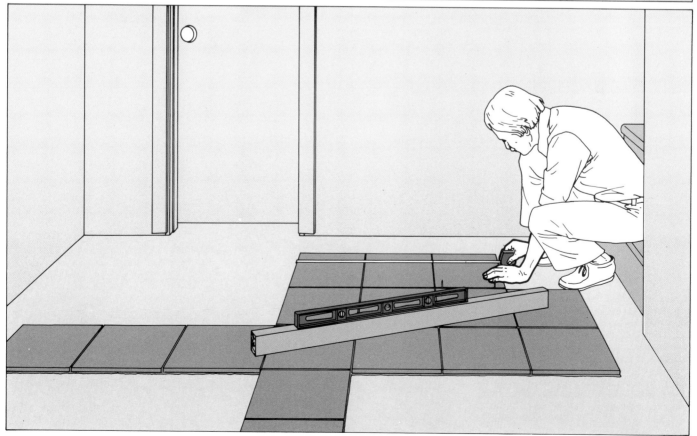

4 Cutting border tiles. Cut stone or thick ceramic tiles, marked to measure *(page 48)*, using an angle grinder fitted with a masonry-cutting disc or blade. Nail two parallel battens, the thickness of the tile and spaced to the same width, to a timber base. Nail another batten across them and support the base on a timber board clamped to sawhorses. Slide the tile between the parallel battens and align the cutting mark with the edge of the top batten. Secure the tile with a cramp and a piece of scrap timber to protect its surface. Using the top batten as a guide, cut the tile a third of the way through *(below, left)*, then tap it with a hammer over the edge of another tile for a clean break. Thin tiles can be cut with a hand cutter and straight-edge, but for large quantities use a mechanical tile cutter *(below, right)*. Push the handle forward to draw the scoring wheel across the surface, then flip the handle back and tap it so the flanges on either side of the wheel strike the tile and snap it along the score line.

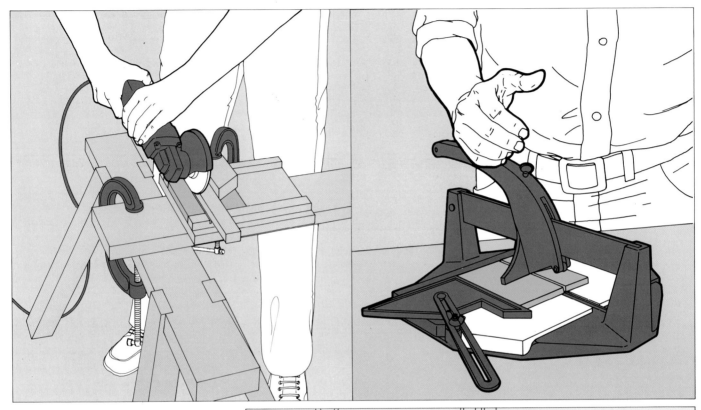

5 Setting a threshold. For hard-tile floors, matching thresholds can be installed in interior doorways. Remove the doorstops with a pry bar, then set the threshold in a bed of adhesive as you would a tile. Stone thresholds must be cut to length by the supplier; ceramic thresholds can be made up with bull-nosed, or bevelled, tiles. Bathroom thresholds should rise 6 mm above the floor to make a dam against spills. Where a hard-tile floor ends at an outside door, install an L-shaped metal threshold that slots under the edge of the tiles.

6 **Grouting between tiles.** Using a squeegee, pack into the spaces between tiles a cement-based grout made from dry pre-mixed powder and water mixed to a partly fluid consistency. Draw the squeegee over each joint, first in one direction, then in the other, crossing the tile edges at a slight angle. Then use a damp cloth to wipe the tiles and recess the grout slightly. As soon as the grout starts to set, clean the film of cement from the tiles by sponging with water. The grey grout made with Portland cement is inconspicuous and does not show dirt; if you wish, add powdered colouring, available from builders' merchants. Some tiles can stain, so it is wise to apply a tile sealer liquid before using coloured grouting.

The Informal Charm of a Flagstone Floor

Flagstone's natural texture, colour and jigsaw-puzzle jointing make it a most intriguing material for use in both patios and hallways. Quarried from the sedimentary stones—limestone, sandstone, bluestone or slate—flagstone comes in a wonderful array of sizes, shapes and colours, although its thickness is generally between 6 and 25 mm. You can buy it or even find pieces of a usable thickness lying at the base of a fragmenting cliff, ready-split and in interesting shapes. From whichever source you obtain your flagstones, always select the pieces with an eye to colour; stones that seem similar when they are seen separately may create too much of a contrast when they are set in the floor side by side.

Because flagstones will be somewhat uneven on both sides, they cannot be laid in the thin-set mortar adhesive which is used for laying tiles. Instead, you should plan to tamp the flagstones into a bed of mortar between 18 and 30 mm thick.

Large stones and thick mortar are too heavy for most suspended timber subfloors. Lay flagstones only at ground level on a sound concrete base.

The aesthetics of a flagstone floor depend mostly on layout, which should be planned in a dry run. Search for pieces with edges sufficiently straight to meet the walls at the border. Fill in by finding larger stones that join approximately with the borders and with one another, even if they leave some sizeable gaps; then look for smaller flagstones to fill in the gaps. Keep the joints between the pieces to no more than 25 mm, allowing some occasional exceptions.

Some stones will need trimming. You can fit the softer kinds of stone, such as sandstone, by chipping with a bricklayer's hammer (or an old claw hammer, since the hammer face may get marred in the process). First, undercut the edge by chipping along its lower side (below), and then chip away the sharp overhang. Cut harder stones by scoring with an angle grinder (opposite page, Step 4), then tapping the score with a hammer and a stone chisel until the stone breaks in two.

Make mortar, using 1 part Portland cement, 4 parts masonry sand and just enough water so that a trowel stuck into the mixture will not fall over. To ensure a good bond between a concrete subfloor and the mortar, apply a latex or epoxy bonding agent, available from building suppliers, to the floor just before trowelling on the mortar.

Lay down mortar for one stone, then brush the underside of the stone with a paste-like mixture of cement and water. Press the stone firmly in place and level it with a rubber mallet. To make sure subsequent stones are roughly level with the first, use a spirit level and a straight length of timber (page 53, Step 3). Grout the joints with mortar, trowelled in and recessed slightly by drawing a piece of pipe along the seam. Mist the floor with water and let it cure for three days under polythene sheeting.

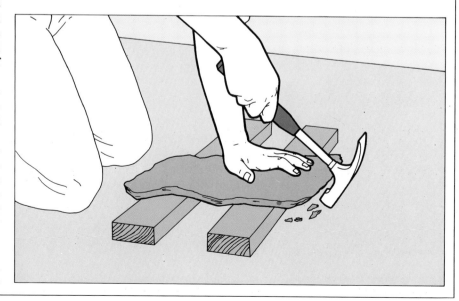

A Concrete Floor with a Smooth Screed Finish

A concrete floor finished with a mortar screed is the best replacement for a rotten or uneven suspended timber floor. Built up in layers from ground level and damp-proofed with a polythene membrane *(below)*, its smooth, dry, durable surface is ideal for ceramic or stone tiles and as a base for a chipboard subfloor *(page 36)*.

The installation of this type of floor requires considerable forethought and planning. The finished floor will be at least 250 mm thick, so check that doorways will not be obstructed or headroom restricted. Underfloor pipes and cables must be either lagged or enclosed in conduits according to the recommendations of the appropriate authorities. Suspended timber floors in adjacent rooms must be ventilated: connect them to airbricks in external walls with 100 mm plastic tubing bedded into the concrete floor foundation.

Before work commences, get together the materials you will need. A builders' merchant will usually deliver everything, but you may have to order the hardcore from a demolition firm. To estimate how many cubic metres of concrete, screed and hardcore you will need, multiply the area to be covered by the thickness of each layer. Order the concrete ingredients in proportions of either 1 part Portland cement to 2 parts concreting sand and 3 parts coarse aggregate, or 1 part cement to 5 parts of 20 mm "all-in" aggregate; for screed, the proportions are 3 parts sharp sand to 1 part cement. Remember that cement must always be kept dry if it is kept in store before use.

For large quantities of concrete, hire an electric or diesel-powered mixer. To mix the first batch of concrete, fill the mixer about two-thirds full with proportionate amounts of the dry ingredients, blend them together, then gradually add water until the mix binds. Once you are sure of the amount of water needed, mix subsequent batches of concrete by adding the dry ingredients to the water.

Wear protective gloves when mixing concrete to avoid skin irritation. If you get concrete in your eyes, bathe them immediately in cold water and see a doctor as soon as possible. After mixing, wash the mixer thoroughly with cold water and clean off splashes from your skin.

To speed the job of spreading the concrete, enlist two helpers to mix and move it to the area being covered. Divide the room into bays about 1 metre wide *(page 59, Step 5)*; to avoid walking on wet concrete, fill the bay furthest from the doorway first then work back towards it. When the concrete has cured—after about two weeks— finish the floor by laying the screed in the same way *(pages 60–61)*.

A properly laid concrete floor requires no maintenance. However, if the screed should crack or crumble with the passage of time—or if you have an old concrete floor that needs resurfacing—you can break up the old screed with an electric hammer or a pick and then lay a new one on the concrete slab. In the case of an old concrete floor that shows signs of damp— usually caused by a faulty membrane—lay a new polythene membrane over the slab and then cover it with a screed between 50 and 65 mm thick.

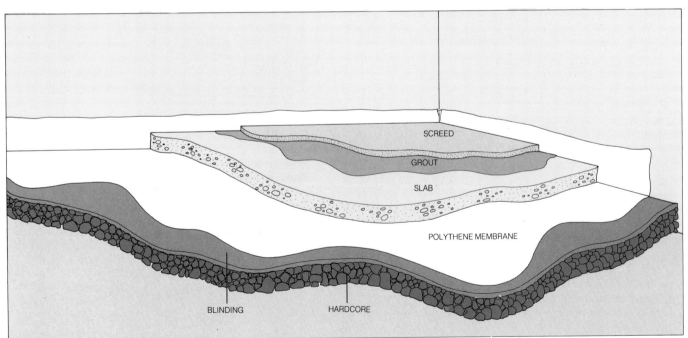

Anatomy of a concrete floor. A solid concrete floor is built up from ground level with several layers of different materials. The base of hardcore or builders' rubble, usually between 100 and 150 mm thick, is topped by a "blinding" layer of sand or hoggin which protects the damp-proof membrane and provides a level surface for the next layer—a concrete slab the same thickness as the hardcore. The surface of the slab is coated with grout to provide a bond with the topmost layer, a fine mortar screed at least 40 mm thick. The edges of the damp-proof membrane lap up the walls above the concrete slab and the screed to provide a continuous barrier against damp.

Laying the Groundwork

1 **Marking finished floor and slab levels.** Clear the site of debris such as pieces of timber, paper or plaster, and protect exposed pipes and wires with lagging or conduits. Using a doorway as a guide, establish the finished floor level so that it corresponds with those in adjoining rooms, and mark the wall 1 metre above it. Draw a continuous line round the room at this level, then measure 1 metre down from this line and draw a line to mark the finished floor level. Beside the doorway, and at each corner, measure down the thickness of the screed from the floor level line, and drive masonry pins into the wall. Tie taut lengths of string between the pins *(right)*; the string marks the level to which the concrete slab will be laid.

In a room with plastered walls, cut away the plaster to about 25 mm above finished floor level before drawing the finished floor level line and setting the slab string.

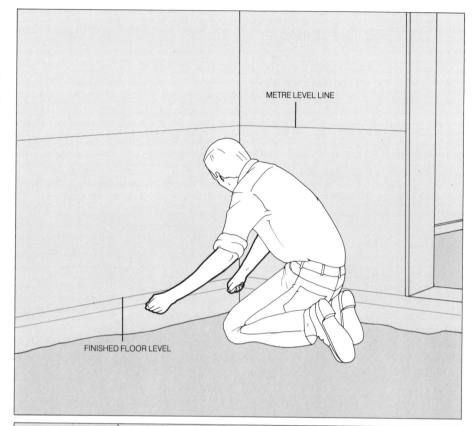

METRE LEVEL LINE

FINISHED FLOOR LEVEL

2 **Laying the hardcore.** Drive wooden pegs into the ground at 1 metre intervals along the wall strings, and across the centre of the room. Hammer the pegs in 100 mm—or the thickness of the concrete slab—below the string line. Starting in the corner of the room furthest from the door, spread hardcore evenly across the room, breaking down large chunks with a sledgehammer. Compact the hardcore with a tamper—a sturdy metal plate on a wooden handle—until it is level with the top of the pegs. Turn jagged edges away from the surface as these might damage the damp-proof membrane. Check that the surface is even by laying a long straightedge between the pegs *(right)*, and adjust where necessary. Remove the pegs, then fill in the spaces they leave with hardcore.

3 **Spreading the blinding.** Shovel sharp sand or hoggin on to the hardcore, then use the back of the shovel to spread it out into an even layer. As you work across the room, tamp down the blinding with a piece of straight-edged timber.

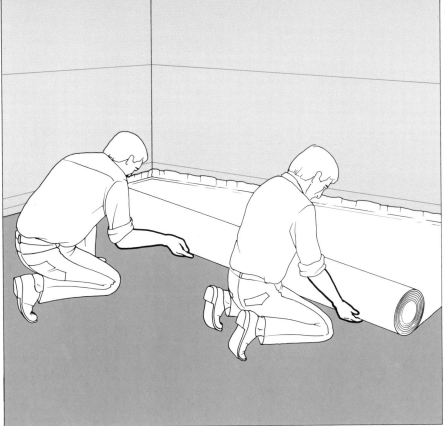

4 **Installing the membrane.** Lay a sheet of 250 micron (1000 gauge) polythene over the blinding, lapping the edges up the walls above the finished floor level line and, for outside walls, the damp-proof course. Pleat the polythene neatly into the corners of the room. Smooth out any bumps or wrinkles, then tuck the turned-up edges behind the string marking the slab level.

If you have to use more than one piece of polythene for the membrane, overlap the joins and seal them with heavy-duty PVC tape.

5 Pouring the concrete. Divide the room into bays about 1 metre wide, using 1.5 to 2 metre lengths of timber 50 mm wide bedded in mortar. Check that the tops of the timber rails are level with the slab strings around the room, then remove the strings. To protect the damp-proof membrane as you work, lay planks down the centre of the first bay to be filled. Starting in the corner furthest from the doorway, tip concrete into the bay until you have enough to fill the first metre or so. Spread the concrete with a shovel until it is roughly level and just proud of the dividing timbers.

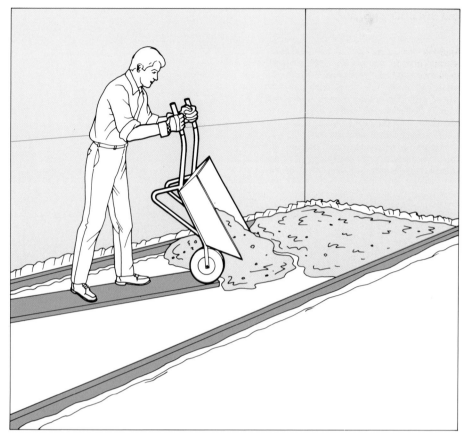

6 Levelling the concrete. Tamp the concrete with a 100 by 50 mm board about 1200 mm long, moving the board with a chopping motion, and gradually drawing it towards you until the surface of the concrete is smooth and flush with the bay dividers.

Continue to lay and level the concrete in this way, removing the planks and the dividers between adjacent bays and filling their indentations as you proceed. When the slab is complete, cover the concrete with damp sacking or plastic sheeting and leave it to cure and harden for about two weeks; if the sacking begins to dry out during this time, sprinkle it with water.

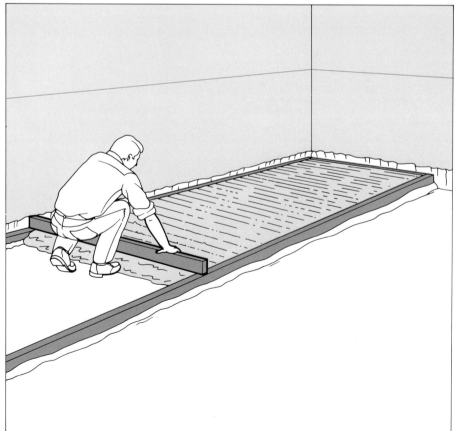

Screeding the Slab

1 Applying the grout. Scrub the concrete with warm water to remove loose surface particles. Prepare a batch of screed *(page 56)*, mixed in the same way as concrete, then make a small quantity of grout by mixing cement and water to a creamy consistency and adding to this a proprietary bonding agent in the proportions recommended by the manufacturer.

Beginning where you laid the first area of concrete for the slab, apply grout to about a square metre of concrete, using a soft brush.

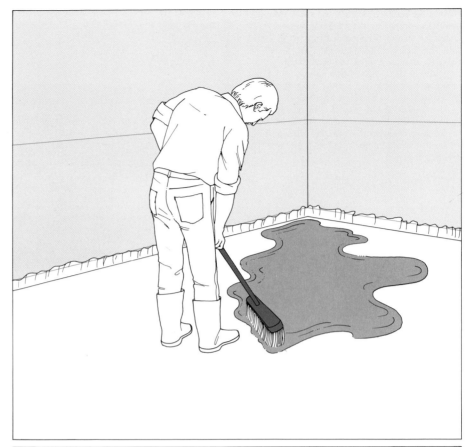

2 Setting the screeding rails. Spread two parallel 100 mm wide strips of screed the length of the grouted area, positioning one 75 mm from the wall and the other about 1 metre from the first. On each strip, lay a metre-long 75 by 37 mm timber screeding rail with its wide face up. Tap the rails with a club hammer to bed them down, then use a spirit level and straightedge to check that both rails are level with the finished floor line marked on the wall.

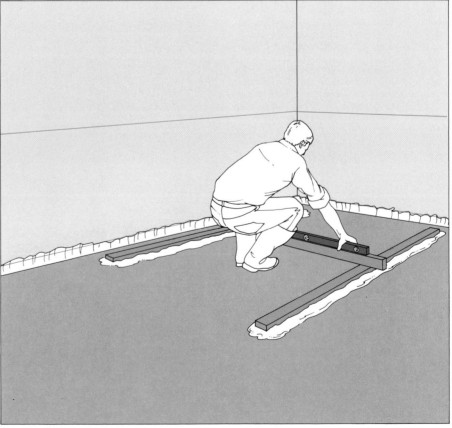

3 **Laying the screed.** Check the consistency of the screed by squeezing a little in your hand; if it is not wet enough to hold its shape without crumbling, adjust the mix. Cover the grouted area with screed and spread it with the shovel until it is slightly proud of the rails. Tamp the screed with the board which was used to level the concrete, then strike off the excess by sliding the board along the rails *(right)*. If the surface is uneven or pitted, add some more screed and repeat the process. Remove the rail nearest to the wall and fill in the gap.

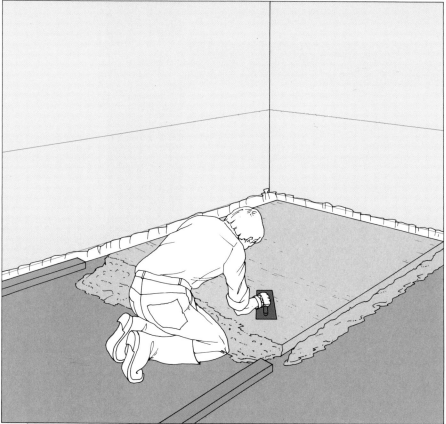

4 **Smoothing the surface.** Skim the surface of the screed with a steel float, using a light circular movement. When it is smooth, grout the next square metre, apply screed and skim it, taking care to erase the join between the two areas. Work round the room following the same pattern you used for laying the slab; as you screed adjoining bays, remove the screeding rails and fill the depressions in the same way.

Leave the screed to dry overnight and then sprinkle it with water, repeating this process over the next two or three days. The floor will be hard enough to walk on after about 24 hours, but you must leave it for at least another two weeks before you lay tiles or cover it with carpet or a chipboard subfloor.

3 The Craftsmanship of Staircases

An iron spiral. This stark, compact spiral staircase is one of several models sold in kit form. Typically, the components include a centre pole, treads that are slotted on to the centre pole from above, balusters and a separate handrail, together with full assembly instructions and all the bolts or other fixing devices required. More elaborate spiral staircases made of hardwood, steel and other materials are also available.

"To make a compleate *Stair-case*, is a curious peece of *Architecture*," wrote the English architect Sir Henry Wotten in 1624. He went on to give stair builders some sage counsel on safety and comfort, recommending that a stairway "have a very liberall *Light*, against all casualtie of *Slippes*, and *Falles*", advising that headroom should "bee large and *Airy*... because a man doth spend much breath in mounting", and stressing the merits of wide treads and an easy slope, "for our *Legges* doe labour more in *Elevation*, than in *Distension*".

Sir Henry's concerns are shared by modern designers—with good reason. More accidents happen on staircases than in baths. By far the greatest causes of staircase accidents are tread defects, steepness and missing handrails. Therefore, the safety problems of maintaining staircases *(pages 64–73)* and building them *(pages 74–93)* centre on the treads, the degree of climb and the handrail.

A slippery tread is a dangerous tread. To increase tread friction, avoid waxing bare wood; instead, cover the wood with abrasive paint or carpet. If infirm persons use a staircase, rubber treads may be advisable. A second tread defect is inadequate depth. When walking downstairs, most adults let their toes overhang the rounded nosing at the front of the tread. If a tread is 250 mm or more deep, the overhang is slight and the tread safe; but every reduction in depth raises the danger that a toe will slip over the nosing. In a well-designed staircase, each tread protrudes over the one below by about 25 mm, gaining tread depth without increasing the distance covered horizontally.

Building regulations require that the steepness, or pitch, of a staircase must not exceed 42 degrees; at that angle there is relatively little danger that a person coming downstairs will fall over. With a tread 250 mm deep and overhanging the one below it by 25 mm, a rise of 175 mm from one tread to the next creates a comfortable slope. Moreover, each step should have exactly the same rise; uneven heights are a factor in many staircase accidents. Missing handrails cause accidents, and the handrails in place must be safe. This again is mostly a matter of dimensions. A handrail should stand 840 mm to 1 metre above the tread nosings and should be narrow enough to be grasped firmly. A balustrade should be strong enough to take the weight of a falling adult, and balusters must be no more than 100 mm apart, so that a young child's head will not pass between them.

Lesser design dangers must also be guarded against: staircases too narrow for two persons to pass, doors that open over treads rather than over landings, improper lighting. And no staircase should run for any great length without a landing, an amenity that is essential, as Sir Henry put it, for "reposing on the way".

Intricate Structures, Simple to Repair

The structure of a staircase goes beyond hammer-and-saw carpentry to involve the stronger and more elegant techniques of joinery, with its generous use of hardwood and ingenious joints. For this reason a properly built staircase is not likely to present major problems.

If the staircase sags or bounces or seems unsafe, the cause is probably settling of the floor under the newel post or at the landing, which throws the staircase out of plumb and level and skews its right-angle joints. Jacking up the floor *(pages 14–21)* may successfully restore an ailing staircase's health, but if the damage is extensive (or if you judge that the original craftsmanship might have been poor) it may be wise to install a new prefabricated staircase *(pages 90–93)*.

The most common problems, however, are relatively manageable ones such as squeaks, broken parts, a wobbly newel post or worn treads. The following pages offer an assortment of solutions to these problems. For many of the repairs you need to know how your staircase was built. Rough staircases, such as outside stairs or basement stairs *(pages 86–89)*, are sometimes made by simpler methods, and metal spiral stairs *(pages 82–85)* are a special case, but among finished interior staircases made of wood there are only two basic types, and these are defined by the way in which the treads are supported.

In most old staircases *(right)*, and also in some new ones built for special purposes, a thick board cut to the shape of the steps runs the length of the flight along the open side. Known as an "open" or "cut" string, this sawtooth-notched length of timber supports the treads and provides surfaces for nailing the risers, the vertical boards between the treads. There may also be a similarly cut board, or "carriage", providing support under the centre of the stairs. Along the wall side of the staircase is a "closed string", a supporting board that is notched, or "housed", 12 mm deep to receive the ends of the treads and risers. Modern prefabricated staircases *(opposite page, above)* are made with closed strings on both sides and do not have carriages unless they are exceptionally wide and require the extra support. Both these types of staircases are named after the string that supports their outer sides: traditional stairs are known as "open string", modern stairs as "closed string".

Except for runs that rise less than 600 mm, open-sided staircases require a post-and-railing fence—an angled balustrade—to provide a handhold. Narrow vertical posts known as balusters are jointed into the handrail and, in traditional staircases, into the ends of the treads. Modern closed-string staircases have a simpler balustrade construction *(pages 74–77)*.

Two precautions are in order when you are repairing staircases. Treads, risers, balusters, newel posts, rails and mouldings are often made of hardwood—usually oak, mahogany or elm—and will split unless pilot holes are bored for all nails and screws. Secondly, glue, often used to repair treads and balusters, will not bond to dried glue; joints must be thoroughly scraped to remove old glue before they can be reassembled. Glue can also mar the finish of any wood, especially hardwood. Use it sparingly. If glue runs on to the wood, wipe it away immediately with a damp cloth, then let the area dry and sand it.

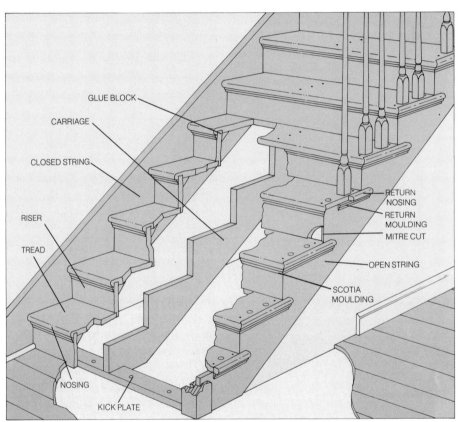

An open-string staircase. In this traditional staircase, an open string with sawtooth cuts for each step runs between floors. On the inner side is a closed string, screwed to the wall and notched with housings for the treads and risers *(opposite page, above)*. A supporting carriage, cut like the open string, runs up the centre of the stairs. At the bottom the strings and carriage fit over a kick plate, a length of timber nailed to the floor to keep them from sliding. The 16 mm risers and the 25 to 28 mm treads are nailed to the carriage and outer string. The bottom of each riser is rebated to receive the back of a tread, and the top of each slots into a housing in the underside of a tread. Glue blocks reinforce joints between treads and risers at the front of each step, and screws through the riser into the tread strengthen the joint at the back. Treads project beyond the risers beneath them—usually by 18 to 25 mm—and end in rounded edges called nosing. The vertical cuts on the open string are mitred to match a mitre at the end of the riser, thus concealing the end grain. A return nosing pinned on the outer end of each tread also hides end-grain. Return moulding at the end and a scotia moulding at the front complete the tread trim.

Labels on illustration: GLUE BLOCK, CARRIAGE, CLOSED STRING, RISER, TREAD, NOSING, KICK PLATE, RETURN NOSING, RETURN MOULDING, MITRE CUT, OPEN STRING, SCOTIA MOULDING

A prefabricated staircase. Cut and assembled—minus the balustrade—in a factory, the staircase now used by most builders employs glue wedges to clamp the ends of the treads and risers in V-shaped housings, which are routed into the sides of the closed strings. The treads and risers here meet in tongue and groove joints, with the treads grooved both at the back and at the underside near the front to accept the tongued risers. Treads are fixed to risers with screws driven up into the risers at the back of each step. Three glue blocks per step strengthen the joint at the front.

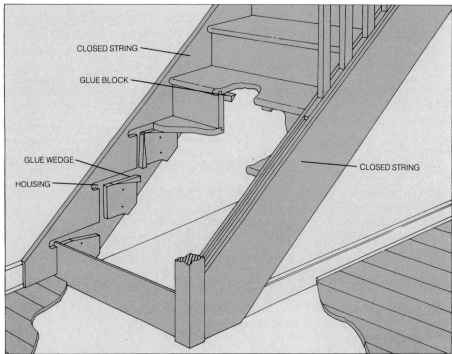

The parts of a balustrade. Structural support for the handrail comes from strong newel posts at the bottom and at the landing. The floor newel has slots called mortises to receive the ends of the handrail and the open string. The base of the newel is often anchored with a steel dowel that runs into a joint or nogging below the floorboards. Landing newels, similarly housed and mortised, are bolted to the trimmer joists *(page 93)*.

The handrail rises to the upper newel in a curved piece called a gooseneck, secured to the handrail with a handrail screw *(inset)*. The wood screw end is screwed into the gooseneck, and the bolt end runs into a shank hole in the end of the handrail. A washer and a nut are attached to the bolt through an access hole bored from underneath the rail. The nut is tightened by driving a nail punch or screwdriver against the notches in the nut. Then the access hole is plugged.

Vertical balusters are installed between treads and the handrail, usually with dowels but sometimes at the bottom with dovetail joints *(page 69, Step 2)*. Often the top dowels are press-fitted into their holes in order to prevent glue from dripping down the balusters.

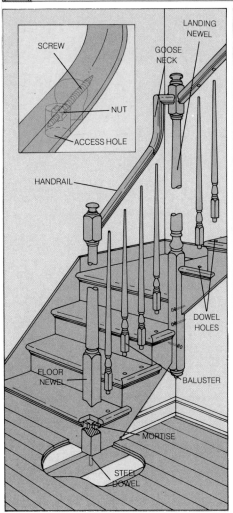

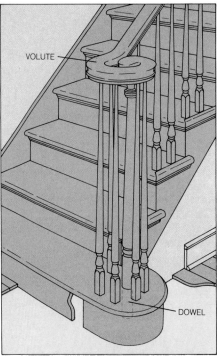

A newel post in a rounded tread. In an adaptation of a traditional form, many staircases use a longer starting tread with a rounded end, which simplifies newel-post installation. The post is set in a hole drilled through the centre of the tread end, and a thick dowel extends to floor level through the curved step end which is generally cut from solid wood or a laminated block. The spiralled end of the handrail, the volute, is glued to a dowel that protrudes up from the newel post. Balusters from the tread end to the volute give further support to the rail.

Silencing a Squeaky Tread

Squeaks, a common problem in older staircases *(page 64)*, are caused by treads that rub against other stair parts when stepped on. The rubbing movement indicates that some portion of the tread has separated slightly from the open string, the carriage or the riser, because of shrinking or warping in these parts; the separated portion is pushed down by a footfall and then springs back up. You can stop tread spring by making the separated portion stay down or, alternatively, by inserting a thin wedge underneath it.

First, you must locate the movement. Use a straightedge to find warps, twists or bows. While a helper is climbing the stairs, listen, watch for rise and fall and—with your hand on the tread—feel for vibration.

After you find the spring you can repair it, if it is minimal, with pairs of angled nails. However, if the tread movement is substantial you will need to use wedges.

Such repairs from the top are usually sufficient. But if you can get to the staircase from underneath you can make a sound and simple repair, preferable because it is invisible, by adding triangular glue blocks *(opposite page, top)* to the joint between the tread and the riser under its front edge, the most common source of squeaks. If the tread is badly warped or humped in the centre, you should rejoin it with a screw through the carriage *(opposite page, centre)*.

Squeaks in modern closed-string staircases *(page 65, above)* are uncommon. If the squeak comes from between a tread and a riser, try nailing or wedging. If it comes from the end of the tread, the glue wedge that supports it has most probably worked loose from shrinkage or the hammering of footfalls. If accessible, replace the wedge *(opposite page, bottom)* with a homemade one cut from 25 mm timber.

Working from Above

Nailing the tread down. Drive two 50 mm lost-head nails into 1.5 mm pilot holes drilled at opposing angles through the tread and into the riser at the point of movement. Ask a helper to stand on the tread during both drilling and nailing. If the squeak comes from the tread ends, angle the holes into the string. Sink the nails with a nail punch and fill the holes with wood filler.

If the tread spring is too great for nails to close, fasten the tread with a No. 8 wood screw, 50 to 63 mm long, driven through a 3 mm shank hole in the tread and into a 1.5 mm pilot hole in the riser *(inset)*. Apply wax or grease to the threads to make the screw turn easily in hardwoods. Glue a piece of dowel into the countersink hole and sand it off level with the tread.

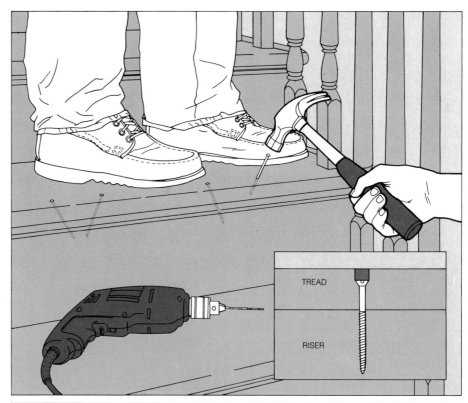

TREAD

RISER

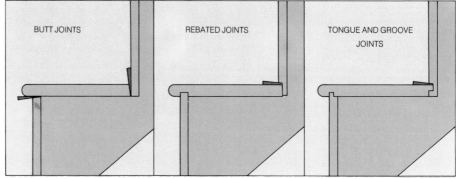

BUTT JOINTS

REBATED JOINTS

TONGUE AND GROOVE JOINTS

Wedging treads tight. Remove the scotia moulding under the tread nose and insert a knife blade into the tread joints to discover the kind of joints used. If they are butt joints, the knife will slip vertically into the joint behind the tread and horizontally under the tread *(above, left)*; if the knife blade stops short, the joints are either rebated or tongue and groove *(above, centre and right)*. Drive narrow, pointed wedges coated with PVA adhesive into the cracks in the directions indicated. Most wedges will tighten a shrunken joint or force the tread down to the carriage or string, and should be driven in hard. The wedge under the tread in a butt joint should prevent a bowed tread from moving by shimming it up; drive the wedges in just enough to stop the squeak without increasing the bow.

Cut wedges off with a trimming knife and replace the scotia moulding. The joints at the back of treads can be covered with quadrant moulding.

Working from Below

Installing glue blocks. Coat PVA adhesive on the two short sides of a triangular block of wood about 75 mm long and cut from 50 mm square timber. Press it into the joint between the tread and the riser, and fasten the block with a panel pin in each direction. Add two or three more blocks. If the joint has old blocks that have come partly unstuck, either install new blocks between them or prise them off, scrape the dried glue on the stair parts down to bare wood and use the new blocks as replacements.

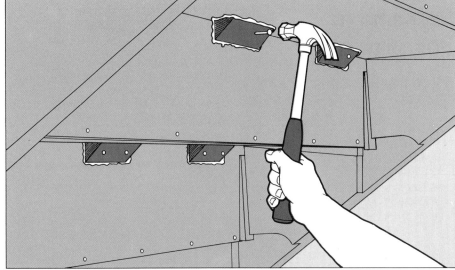

Installing a screw through the carriage. About 50 mm below the tread, chisel a shallow notch into the carriage and with a helper standing on the tread drill a 3 mm pilot hole angled at about 30 degrees through the corner of the carriage and 12 mm into the tread. Enlarge the hole through the carriage with a 6 mm drill. Spread a bead of PVA adhesive along both sides of the joint between the tread and the carriage and, with the helper off the tread, work the adhesive into the joint, using a putty knife. With the helper standing on the tread again, install a No. 12 wood screw 63 to 75 mm long.

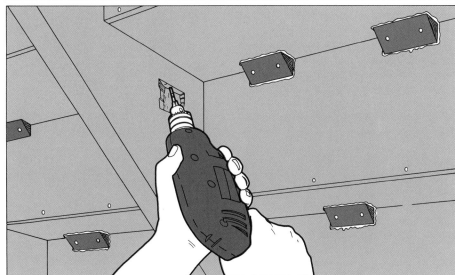

Wedges for a Prefabricated Stair

Replacing loose wedges. Split out the old wedge with a chisel, and pare dried glue and splinters from the housing. Cut a new wedge to fit within 25 mm of the riser, making sure that the grain runs the length of the wedge. Coat the housing, the bottom of the tread and the top and bottom of the wedge with PVA adhesive. Hammer the wedge snugly into the housing, tap it along the side to force it against the notch face, then hit the end a few more times to jam the wedge tightly under the tread.

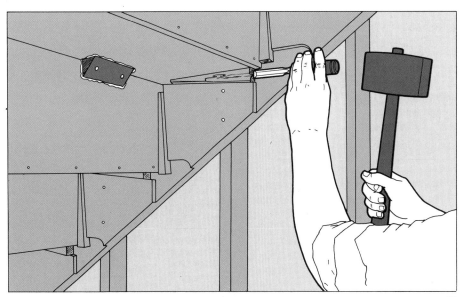

Repairing a Balustrade

With its graceful moulded railing and its row of slender balusters, the stairway balustrade, essential for safety, is also the set piece of the joiner's art in many homes. Thus a broken baluster or a shaky railing affects not only the safety of the stairway but also its appearance.

A baluster that is merely loose can be tightened with glue, nails or small wedges, but if cracked or badly scraped or dented it should be replaced. First of all, determine how your balusters are fastened. Square-topped balusters usually join the handrail by fitting into a shallow groove just as wide as the baluster is thick. Blocks of wood called fillets are nailed into the grooves between balusters. In some staircases, such balusters may also end in the groove of a base rail that lies on top of a closed string *(opposite page below, Steps 1 and 2)*.

Turned balusters rounded clear to the top go into holes in the handrail. At the bottom, if they do not overlap the return nosing (the piece that hides the end-grain of the tread), they are also dowelled, even though they may have square ends. But square-ended balusters that land on the tread slightly overlapping the return nosing are probably joined to the tread by a dovetail joint, and you will have to remove the return nosing not only to be sure but also to make the replacement. Save the broken baluster and use it as a pattern for a new one. If you cannot find a match at a timber yard, you will have to locate a joiner who will turn one. You can buy a square-bottomed replacement for a dovetailed baluster and cut the dovetail yourself, using the principles shown on pages 71–72, but you can also simply pin a dowelled baluster into the dovetailed tread with a nail.

The cause of a weak and wobbly handrail is often poor fastenings in the bottom newel post, loosely cut mortises or broken tenons on the string. The cure is to reinforce the post with screws driven into the string from the front of the newel. For posts in rounded-end treads, as shown on page 65, you can run a bolt up through the floor into the foot of the post.

Replacing a Dowelled Baluster

1 **Removing the damaged baluster.** Saw the baluster in two and sharply twist the bottom piece with a pipe wrench to break the glue joint at the base. Remove the top piece; if it is stuck or glued, use the wrench. If the joints do not break, saw the baluster flush, using cardboard on the tread to protect it from the saw. Drill out the dowel ends with spade bits the size of the dowels on the new baluster.

With a folding rule held against the high edge of the dowel hole in the handrail *(inset)*, measure to the tread. Cutting from the top, shorten the new baluster to this length plus 12 mm. Saw the bottom dowel to a 5 mm stub.

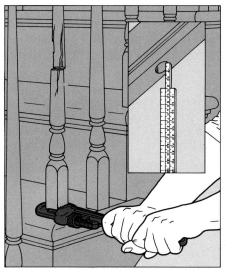

2 **Installing the new baluster.** Smear glue in the tread hole, angle the top dowel into the handrail hole and pull the bottom of the baluster across the tread, lifting the handrail about 6 mm. Seat the bottom dowel in the tread hole. If the handrail will not lift, bevel the top dowel where it binds against the side of the hole.

A Dovetailed Baluster

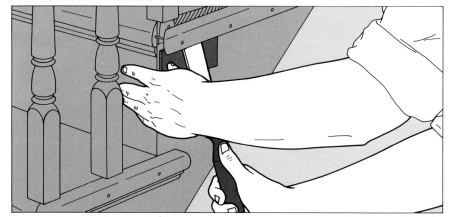

1 **Removing the return nosing.** Use an old chisel to crack the joints, then prise off return moulding and return nosing, protecting the string with a timber scrap *(above)*. Saw through the old baluster, then hammer it out of the dovetail.

2 **Nailing in the new baluster.** Insert the top of a cut-to-length dowelled baluster into the handrail hole and set its base in the tread dovetail where the old baluster was, shimming behind the dowel if this is necessary to bring the new baluster into line with the others. Drill a pilot hole through the dowel into the tread, and drive a nail through the hole. Replace the return nosing and return moulding, driving lost-head nails through the old holes, and fill over the nail heads with wood filler.

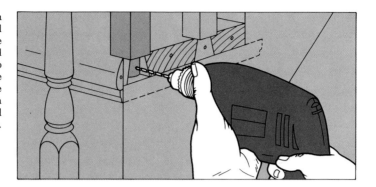

A Filleted Baluster

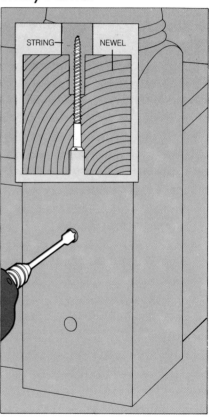

1 **Taking out the old baluster.** With a chisel, split the fillets below the butt of the old baluster and above the top into several pieces and prise them out. Drive each end of the baluster towards the chiselled-out grooves, breaking the nailing, and remove the baluster. Scrape old glue from the grooves. Obtain the angle for the new baluster ends and fillets using a sliding bevel between an adjacent baluster and fillet. Mark the angle on the new baluster and saw it to length.

Tightening a Shaky Newel

STRING NEWEL

Fixing the screws. With a 12 mm spade bit and an electric drill, drill two countersink holes, one above the other, 20 mm deep into the front of the newel post and aimed at the end of the string. Extend them through the newel with a hole the diameter of the shank of a No. 12 screw. Using a screwdriver, drive two No. 12 screws at least 100 mm long through the pilot holes and into the string *(inset)*. Plug the holes with dowelling or cross-grain pellets.

To steady a newel set in a rounded-end tread, drive two nails through the flooring short distances from the newel. From beneath, measure from the nail points to locate the bottom of the newel dowel. Drill a shank and pilot holes and install a 6 mm coach screw 75 mm long. Pull out nails and fill holes with wood filler.

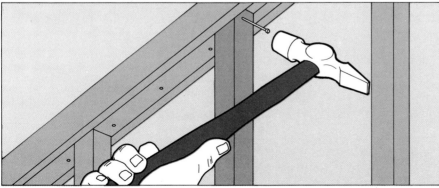

2 **Fastening the new baluster.** Set the baluster against the existing fillets and toenail two lost-head nails through each end—into the handrail and base rail. Start the nails where the new fillets will hide them, and punch the heads.

Measure each new fillet, mark the angle cuts with the sliding bevel and cut with a mitre box. Coat the backs and sides with PVA adhesive and attach them in the handrail and base rail grooves with panel pins.

Retreading a Staircase

Subject to heavy traffic, stair treads suffer scrapes, dents and stains, and may wear unevenly or split. In any type of staircase you can readily replace individual treads, except for a rounded-end starting tread which involves dismantling the handrail and replacing the newel post. For an uncarpeted staircase, try to match the replacement material with the original. For a tread that is to be covered, use a section of window board—which is sold with one edge already rounded—or cut a length of softwood to fit, and round off the outer edge with a plane and abrasive paper.

Removing a tread is best tackled from above, as described on this page, but if you have no access to the underside of the staircase you must take care to avoid dislodging the wedges in closed-string housings. If a wedge is lost, support the new tread with a cleat cut from 50 by 25 mm timber, screwed to the string so that its top edge is level with the underside of the tread.

Removing the Old Tread

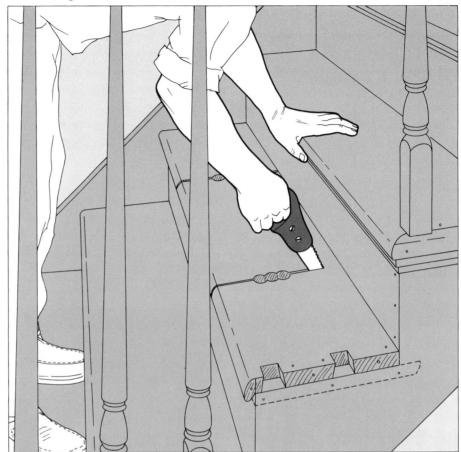

1 **Cutting up the old tread into thirds.** After taking off the balusters *(page 68)* and the mouldings, drill starting holes for a saw and cut across the tread in two places, nicking the edges of the risers in front and behind, but stopping the cut before damaging their exposed surfaces.

2 **Splitting out the sections.** Drive a chisel into the middle third over the riser, so that the nosing breaks off without damaging the riser tongue. Working backwards over the middle, split off more pieces. Prise the last couple of centimetres or so gently away from the screws that hold it to the back riser. Hammer the chisel sideways into the ends of the other thirds, splitting around nails, and pull out the pieces. Remove all nails and knock back protruding screws.

Saw the new tread to length and width. If your staircase has rebated or tongue and groove joints between treads and risers, make allowance in trimming the tread to width and cut rebates or tongues and grooves on the tread, or ask a joiner to do it for you.

Putting in the New Tread: On an Open Stair

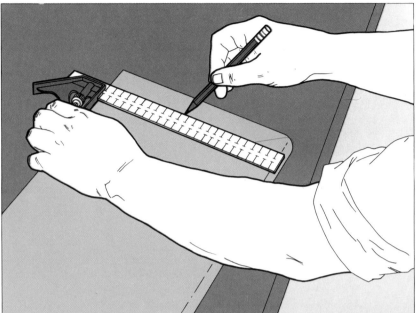

1 **Laying out the nosing cuts.** With a combination square, mark the cuts for the return nosing on the outside end of the new tread. First draw a 45-degree line in from the front corner of the tread for the mitre cut, then lay out a crosscut the width of the nosing.

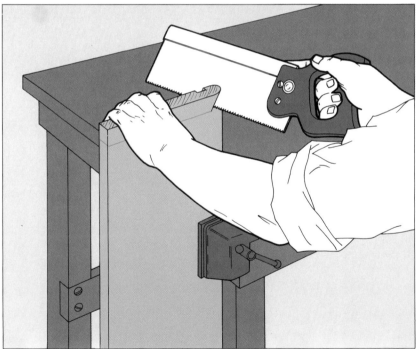

2 **Sawing the cuts.** Cut along the 45-degree line with a tenon saw, then crosscut with a fine-toothed handsaw. Alternatively, you can turn the tread face side down and make the long cut with a jigsaw, using a batten clamped to the tread as a guide. Smooth the cuts with a bullnose plane and a chisel.

3 **Laying out dovetail mortises.** With the tread temporarily in place, use a plumb bob to mark the point directly beneath the centre of a handrail hole. Angle the upper end of the baluster into the hole, hold the bottom against the tread end centred on the plumb-bob mark, and scribe the dovetail angles. With a square, extend the lines on to the top and bottom of the tread, and connect them with lines as far in as the thickness of the dovetail. Repeat for the other baluster.

If the balusters are dowelled into the treads, use the mark as the centre for dowel holes.

4 **Sawing out the dovetails.** Cut the sides of the dovetails just inside the marks with a tenon saw, then cut the back with a coping saw. If necessary, straighten saw cuts by paring with a chisel.

If the balusters are dowelled, drill holes of the dowel diameter 9 mm deep. Use an electric drill fitted with a spade bit or brace and bit.

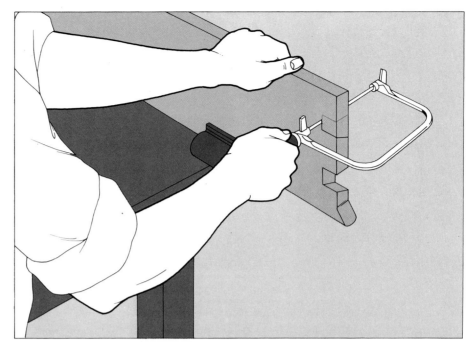

5 **Securing the new tread.** Spread generous beads of PVA adhesive along the tops of the riser and open string, and into the housing of the wall string. Slide the tread into place, then drill three evenly spaced pilot holes through the tread into the riser. Fix with 37 mm No. 8 screws, countersinking their heads, and fill the holes with wood filler. Keep traffic off the tread for about an hour to let the adhesive set. Replace the balusters, the return nosing and the mouldings, following the directions given on pages 68–69.

6 **Fastening from underneath.** If you can reach the underside of the staircase, drill pilot holes through the riser into the tread and fix with 37 mm No. 8 screws. Use glue blocks *(page 67)* along the joint between tread and riser.

Putting In the New Tread: On a Closed Stair

1 **Finding the length of the new tread.** Measure from the face of one string across the staircase into the housing of the other. Subtract a few millimetres to leave some play, and cut the new tread to this length. If the front riser was tongued or rebated into the old tread, chisel and plane it flush with the underside of the tread. If the back riser was tongued into the back of the tread, carefully remove the riser tongue with a chisel so that the new tread will slide into place.

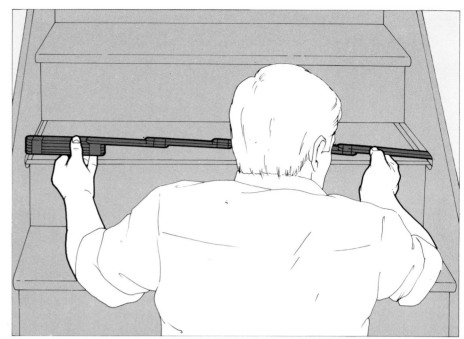

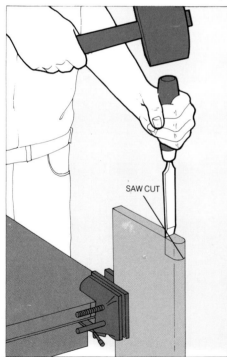

SAW CUT

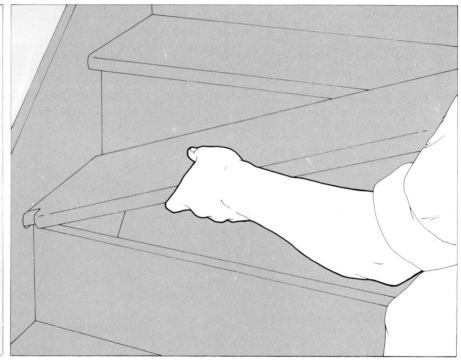

2 **Notching the nosing.** Using a tenon saw and a chisel, make a notch in one of the front corners of the new tread. The distance from the end of the tread to the saw cut should be equal to the depth of the housings in the strings; the chisel split should be made as far back from the nosing as the amount of overhang of the tread above, plus 10 mm for play. Save the cut-out scrap of nosing.

3 **Installing the tread.** Apply PVA adhesive to the housings and to the top of the riser and back edge of the tread. Holding the uncut end of the tread angled upwards, insert the notched end into its housing. The notch will make it possible for you to pull the tread far enough forwards to avoid hitting the nose of the tread above. Lower the tread tight against the back riser, then slide it sideways until the tread notch is revealed. With glue and a nail through a pilot hole, fasten the scrap of nosing which you have saved into the tread notch. Centre the tread, drill pilot holes and fix the tread to the riser with 37 mm No. 8 screws (*opposite page, Steps 5 and 6*).

Replacing a Balustrade: a Facelift for Your Stairs

An unattractive old balustrade, or one that requires more than the simple repairs demonstrated on pages 68–69, may be worth replacing entirely. On a traditional open-string staircase *(page 64)*, which has its dowelled or dovetailed balusters individually measured and fitted for each cutaway step, this job is best left to the professional. The closed-string staircase, however, a design that is commonly found in both old and new houses, can easily be fitted with the type of balustrade which is described on these pages.

In a modern closed-string balustrade, balusters are slotted into grooves in the underside of the handrail and in a base rail that is screwed to the string. Wooden fillets fitted into the grooves between the balusters ensure even spacing. These components, together with replacement newel posts, can all be ordered from a staircase manufacturer, but builders' merchants

and larger D.I.Y. shops also stock a range of parts used for this work.

Staircase manufacturers generally provide a handrail and newel posts that fit together with traditional mortise and tenon joints. The newel posts will already have been mortised at the factory, but you will have to cut tenons on the handrail to fit *(page 76, Steps 4 and 5)*.

You will also have to cut holes in the old newel post bases to receive the spigots of the replacement posts *(opposite page, Step 2)*. If the bases of the newel posts are so wobbly that they cannot be repaired *(page 69)*, you must get a professional joiner to make and install new ones.

Like the handrail, new balusters are supplied square ended and must be cut to length, their ends angled to the pitch of the stairs *(page 77, Step 7)*. When you have measured and cut the first one precisely it will serve as a model for the others.

When preparing the old newel bases to receive the new posts, take care not to cut them off too close to the floor—according to building regulations, the handrail, when fitted to the replacement newel top, must be at least 840 mm above the treads. Open landings, like open-sided staircases, must also be protected by balustrading, but here the minimum height for the handrail is set at 900 mm. Spaces between individual balusters, on both staircases and landings, must not be more than 100 mm. Spacing fillets are sold ready-to-use and cut to a legally acceptable length.

The balustrade which is described on these pages is for a single flight of stairs with one straight handrail, but fittings for more complex designs are readily available. A spiral volute at the base of a handrail or a curving gooseneck at the top *(page 65)* are standard ornamental accessories for staircases.

Anatomy of a balustrade. This balustrade for a closed-string staircase consists of two newel posts, a series of equal-sized balusters, and a grooved handrail and base rail into which the balusters are slotted. The handrail is secured to the newel posts with mortise and tenon joints, and the base rail is fitted over the string and secured with screws. Timber spacing fillets are slotted into the handrail and base rail grooves between the balusters. The upper parts of the newel posts are shown separated from the bases; when replacing an old balustrade, the existing newel bases can usually be retained. Each newel post is topped with a decorative cap.

At the top of the stairs, the balustrade doubles back on itself with the aid of a horizontal turn, an elbow section of handrail that is attached to the rail along the landing with a double-threaded handrail screw.

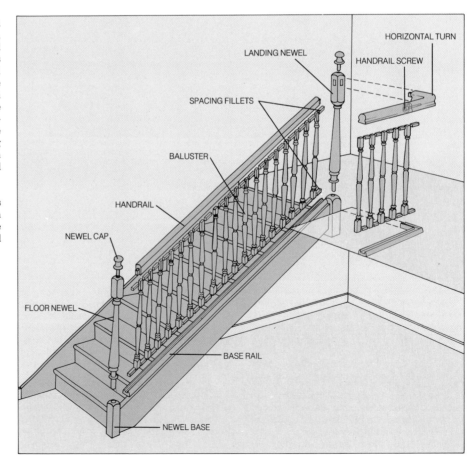

Assembling the Balustrade

1 Cutting the old newel. Determine where to saw off the top of your old newel post by holding the replacement top against it at the correct height for the new handrail. Mark where the top of the spigot begins *(right)* and square a cutting line on the old newel at this point. Carefully saw off the top of the old post.

2 Gouging out the stump. Set a compass to the radius of the newel spigot and, with the point in the exact centre of the sawn-off surface, draw a circle on the newel base. Draw another, concentric circle with a diameter 10 mm smaller than the first. In the gap between the circles, drill a series of 5 mm holes to the same depth as the newel spigot. Using a mallet and scribing gouge, chisel out the area within the outer circle. Work carefully towards the centre of the hole, making sure that its sides are vertical. When the newel spigot fits perfectly, sand and chamfer round the top and corners of the stump to ensure a smooth transition between the old and new sections of post.

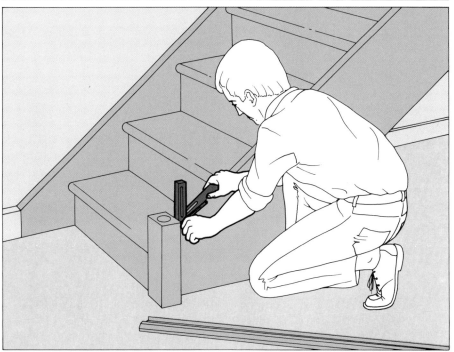

3 Cutting and fixing the base rail. Use a sliding bevel to determine the angle between the string and the newel posts *(right)*. Carefully measure the length of base rail you will need, then make a mark at each end of the section of rail with the bevel set to the same angle and cut along these two lines. Lay the cut length of base rail beside the handrail and use it as a template to mark the lines for the shoulder of the tenon on the top and sides of each end of the handrail. Fix the base rail to the string with 32 mm No. 8 countersunk screws at 300 mm intervals.

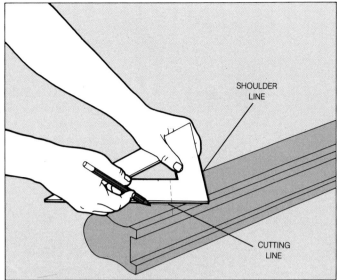

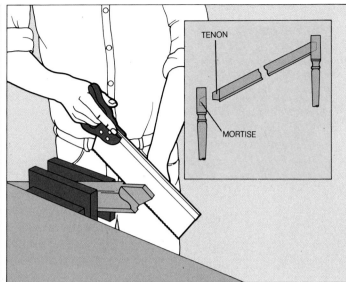

4 Marking and cutting the handrail. Parallel to the shoulder line which you marked on the lower end of the handrail *(page 75, Step 3)*, mark a cutting line at a distance slightly less than the depth of the newel-post mortise towards the end of the rail. Then draw a line to the edge of the rail at right angles to the bottom end of the shoulder line, so that it intersects the cutting line *(above)*. Cut along these two lines with a tenon saw.

5 Cutting the tenon. Using a combination square or mortising gauge, mark two parallel lines along the top and end of the rail, measured and centred to match the newel-post mortise. Cut down these lines *(above)*, stopping at the shoulder line, then cut across the shoulder line from each side of the handrail. Fit the tenon into the mortise; if necessary, adjust the shoulder line at the other end of the rail for a perfect fit. Prepare the upper tenon, using the same technique, so that it is a mirror image of the first *(inset)*.

6 Securing the newels and handrail. Apply PVA adhesive to the spigot of the floor newel post and push it into the prepared hole in the newel base. With an assistant steadying the other end, glue the lower end of the handrail to the floor newel at the mortise and tenon joint, then glue the top of the assembly—the rail to the landing newel, followed by the newel into its base. Check that both posts are exactly plumb, then brace them in position with battens pinned to the base rail and tread nosings. Allow 24 hours for the glue to set and remove the battens.

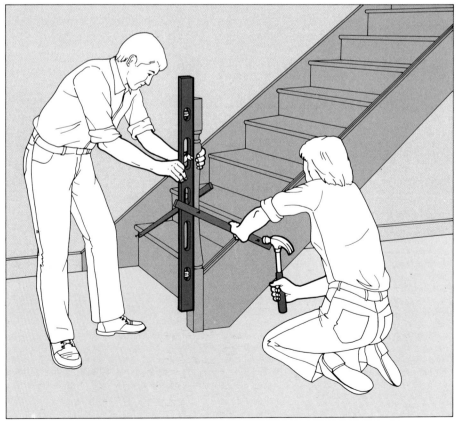

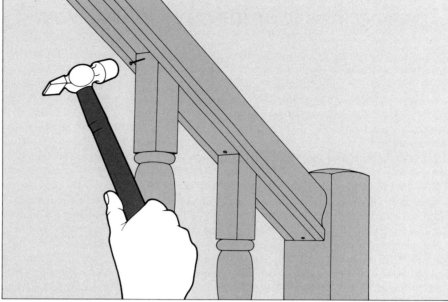

7 **Preparing the balusters.** With a sliding bevel set to the pitch of the stairs, mark the first baluster at top and bottom and then saw it to length; remember to allow for the depth of the grooves in both the base rail and the handrail. Make sure that this baluster is vertical when slotted in position, then use it as a template for the remaining balusters *(above)*.

8 **Fitting the balusters.** Slot the balusters and spacing fillets into place along the length of the base rail, halve the space left between the last baluster and the landing newel and cut four of the fillets to this length. Starting at the bottom of the stairs, slot one cut spacing fillet into the groove of the base rail and another into the underside of the handrail immediately above; use 25 mm panel

pins to secure the fillets. Using 37 mm pins and PVA adhesive, glue and skew-nail the first baluster into both the base rail and the handrail. Continue up the staircase in the same way, alternating balusters with uncut spacers. Secure the two remaining cut fillets between the final baluster and the landing newel. Glue decorative caps into the tops of the newel posts.

How to Join Sections of Handrail

Installing a handrail screw. Tap a panel pin a few millimetres into the centre of one end of a section of handrail. Snip the head of the pin off with a pair of pincers, then carefully align the two sections of rail and push them together so that the headless pin is forced into the end of the second section. Pull the sections apart and remove the pin with a pair of pincers. Drill a pilot hole into the pin hole of one section for the wood screw end of the handrail screw *(right)*. Into the corresponding point of the other section, drill a hole large enough to take the bolt end.

Next drill an access hole, 25 to 32 mm in diameter, into the underside of the section of rail that will take the bolt *(inset)*. Locate this hole so that the end of the bolt will protrude approximately half way across the resulting opening; it must be deep enough for the nut to turn freely on the end of the bolt. Fix the wood screw end into the pilot hole, turning it with an adjustable wrench if necessary. Push the protruding bolt into the other section, slip the washer and nut over the end of it through the access hole, and tighten the nut with a nail punch or screwdriver until the two rail ends fit tightly together. Block the access hole with a timber plug.

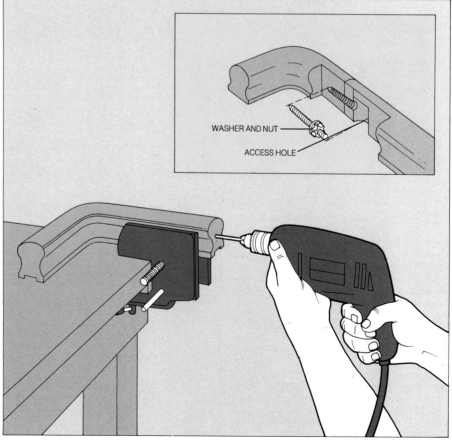

WASHER AND NUT

ACCESS HOLE

Opening the Floor for a New Stairway

If valuable attic storage space is accessible only if you balance on a chair, if you must tiptoe through an adjoining bedroom to get to an upstairs study, if you can reach your basement only by trudging through rain and cold to an exterior door—you know you need a stairway. The first step is to create an access hole in the upper floor—a stair opening with new framing to do the work of the structural timbers you cut out.

Since the addition of new stairs will change the layout of two floors, framing the opening requires forethought. Try to locate the stairs so that existing walls will not have to be moved or demolished to accommodate the new construction; you will need clearance of at least the width of the stairs between the top or bottom tread and a facing wall in order to provide turning space for entering or leaving the stairs. Also try to position the new stairs to avoid interference with water pipes or electrical wiring. And if you can plan the stairs so the longer sides of the opening run parallel to the joists (below) you will simplify the framing—as many as six joists may have

to be cut if the opening runs the other way.

Consult your building control officer at an early stage in your planning. Building regulations specify minimum dimensions for both the width and the headroom of stairways—factors that determine the size of a stair opening. If your stairway leads up to a single room other than a kitchen or a living room, it can be as narrow as 600 mm; in most other cases, 800 mm is the legal minimum width for a staircase.

The length of a conventional stair opening must be sufficient to provide adequate clearance between the stairs and the ceiling overhead. A minimum of 2 metres is required by the building regulations, but remember that greater clearance is advantageous—to accommodate tall people and to simplify the job of moving furniture.

How the opening is measured and how it is marked depends on the type of staircase to be installed. For a straight flight, follow the procedure for a simple closed-string staircase (page 86); the instructions for a spiral staircase and a loft ladder are given on pages 82–85. However, openings for all

types of stairs are cut and reinforced in essentially the same way, following the basic techniques illustrated on these pages for a basement stairway.

When you have established the dimensions of the opening required, add on at least 50 mm all round to allow room for making good after the stairs have been installed. To cut the opening, you will have to remove some flooring, cut through joists and—for all but an unfinished basement, shown here—remove sections of ceiling. To make good afterwards, use scraps of ceiling material to patch areas where the trimmers and trimming joists are exposed. Hide the edges of plaster and flooring with a timber or plywood "apron" nailed to the inside of the opening. Install nosing, available from timber merchants, round the upper edges of the opening for an attractive finish (page 93).

An unprotected stair opening is both dangerous and illegal. Your work is incomplete until you have installed a balustrade (pages 74–77) or simple handrail (page 89) round the edge.

Anatomy of a stair opening. For most openings where the long sides run parallel to the joists, remove portions of two joists and use joist hangers to fasten double lengths of timber, known as trimmers, to the cut ends. The trimmers, which should be the same height and thickness as the joists, are also connected by joist hangers to trimming joists on the sides of the opening. On the right in this example, the trimming joist consists of a new joist fastened to an existing one; on the left, it is made up of two new joists installed between existing floor joists to narrow the width of the opening to the dimensions required for the stairway. For an opening next to a masonry wall, the trimmers can be supported at one side by the wall itself (page 81, below).

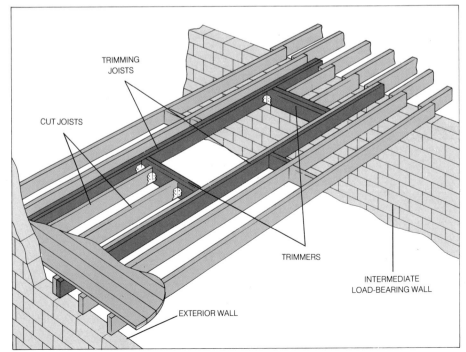

TRIMMING JOISTS

CUT JOISTS

TRIMMERS

INTERMEDIATE LOAD-BEARING WALL

EXTERIOR WALL

1 **Supporting the floor.** Mark the planned opening on the underside of the floor, allowing at least 50 mm all round for making good. Locate the opening as described on page 86 for most stairways, and on page 82 for loft ladders and spiral staircases. Double the joists on each long side of the opening *(pages 16–17)* and then install an adjustable prop and supporting beam *(pages 14–15)* about 500 mm beyond each end. Drill holes up through the floor at each corner.

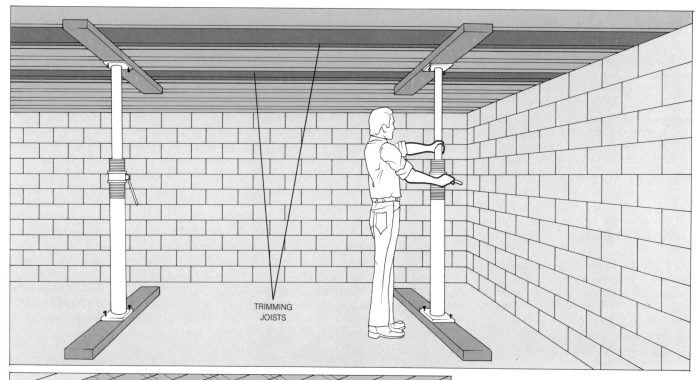

TRIMMING
JOISTS

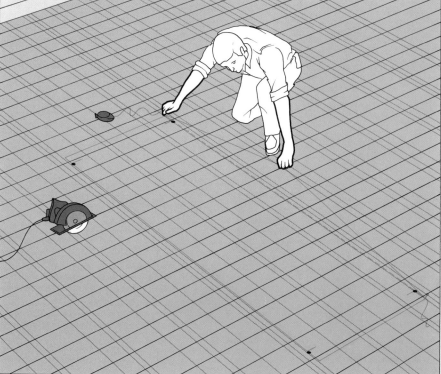

2 **Cutting the opening.** On the upper floor, locate the holes at the corners of the planned opening and measure 100 mm beyond each end to allow for the thickness of the trimmers *(page 81, Step 5)*. Snap four chalk lines to mark the dimensions of the extended opening. Saw along the two sides of the opening that are at right angles to the floorboards, then saw along the two sides parallel to the floorboards.

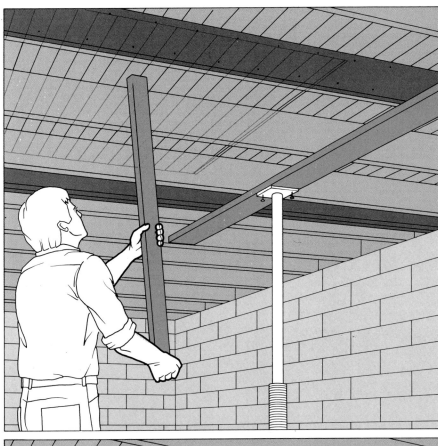

3 Removing the boards. To loosen the boards from the joists, pound upwards with a length of timber along the sides of each joist under the sawn section *(left)*. Then, working from above, use a crowbar to complete the job.

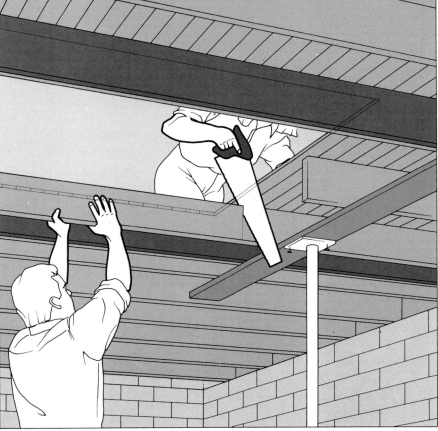

4 Cutting the joists. Saw the joists flush with the opening while a helper supports each joist from underneath to prevent it from pinching the saw as you cut. The cut sections can then be used to make the double trimmers required to complete the framing *(page 78, below)*; cut two lengths to fit between the trimming joists at each end of the opening and fasten them together with coach bolts or 100 mm round-wire nails arranged in a staggered pattern.

5 **Installing the trimmers.** Nail 100 mm joist hangers to each end of a double trimmer. At one end of the opening, butt a trimmer against the ends of the cut joists, bringing its top edge level with the top of the adjoining timbers *(below)*. Nail the joist hangers to the trimming joists, using all the nail holes in the hangers. Slip 50 mm joist hangers on to the cut joists from below and nail them to both the cut joists and the trimmer. Finally, nail the trimmer to the cut joist ends with two 150 mm round-wire nails into each end. Install the other double trimmer in the same way.

An Opening Next to a Masonry Wall

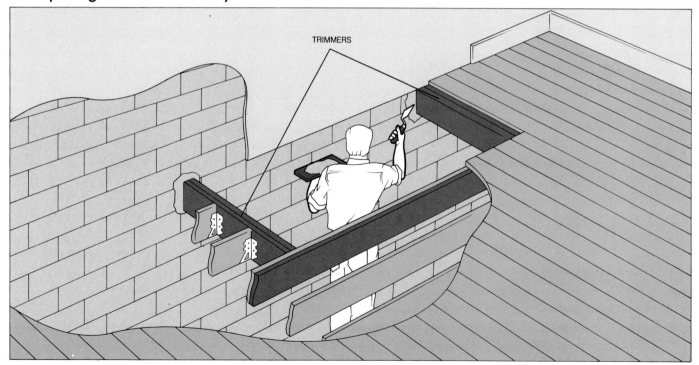

TRIMMERS

Setting the trimmers in the wall. In a basement staircase alongside a masonry wall, trimmers framing the ends of the opening can be supported by the wall itself. With a bolster and club hammer, chop holes in the wall 100 mm deep *(page 16)* to house the ends of the double trimmers. Insert the trimmers into the holes; fix them to the cut joists with round-wire nails and to the trimming joists with joist hangers *(Step 5, above)*. Wedge pieces of tile or slate under the trimmer ends, then make good the wall with mortar and scraps of slate or tile *(page 17)*.

Two Space-Savers: Loft Ladders and Spiral Stairs

Not every house has enough space for a full flight of stairs to an attic or basement, or an additional flight between main floors. However, even the most cramped floor plans can accommodate the two staircases shown here and overleaf. A loft ladder pulls down from the ceiling to provide access to attic storage space, then folds back into the attic when not in use. A spiral staircase not only adds style and beauty to a home, but also takes up less space than a conventional staircase.

Made of aluminium or timber, loft ladders are sold as pre-assembled units by department stores, hardware shops and D.I.Y. centres. One of the most common types consists of hinged sections which can be folded together and tucked out of sight behind a trap door *(below and opposite)*. Other loft ladders have sections which slide on top of one another or compress together like a concertina when not in use. Spiral stairs made of hardwood, cast iron, aluminium or steel are available in kit form from large timber merchants or staircase manufacturers.

Both loft ladders and spiral stairs require stairwell openings *(pages 78–81)* as specified by the manufacturers. It may be possible to install a ladder without any change to an existing opening. If not, you can either cut a new opening or enlarge the existing one—the basic procedure is the same. Where a joist crosses the opening, this must be cut and trimmers inserted.

Before ordering a loft ladder, make sure that there is enough clearance and headroom for the model you have in mind. Clearance, which is measured horizontally on the floor directly beneath the opening, is the amount of space needed to unfold the ladder. Headroom is the space needed above the ceiling to accommodate the ladder when it is folded away. Remember to make allowance for the supporting hardware and, if one is fitted, the handrail.

Ordering a spiral staircase requires a few more measurements. First, determine the staircase diameter and the location best suited to your floor plans. Spiral kits come in a range of overall widths, from 915 to 2440 mm, but the minimum width is not recommended—carrying even small items is difficult on a staircase which is less than 1220 mm wide. Find the most comfortable point to step on and off the stairs at both levels, and decide whether you prefer a stair that is climbed clockwise or anticlockwise. Check with your local planning authority that the staircase will not contravene the building regulations.

When ordering a spiral staircase, you must also specify the exact height of the stair from finished floor to finished floor. To get an accurate measurement, drill a 3 mm hole through the upper floor, feed in a plumb line and attach a plumb bob to the end of the line. Drop the plumb bob to the floor below, then measure the line.

Draw a sketch to accompany your order, indicating the diameter and height of the staircase, the preferred entry and exit direction on each floor and the location of adjoining walls or other obstructions. The manufacturer will help you to determine the number and size of treads for either a full spiral (360 degrees) or a three-quarter turn (270 degrees); instructions for positioning and securing the treads will be supplied with the kit.

If the staircase is to rest on a timber floor, double the joists beneath the centre pole *(page 16)*. If the pole falls between joists, double the joists on either side.

Installing a Loft Ladder

1 Attaching the stairs. After cutting and preparing the joists *(page 78–81)*, position the loft ladder in the opening. Unfold the top section of the ladder, then secure the frame to the joists and trimmers with 75 mm No. 12 screws or 100 mm round-wire nails. To hold the ladder in place while drilling and fixing, support the short ends of the frame on top of two 50 by 50 mm battens cut to the height of the ceiling above the floor.

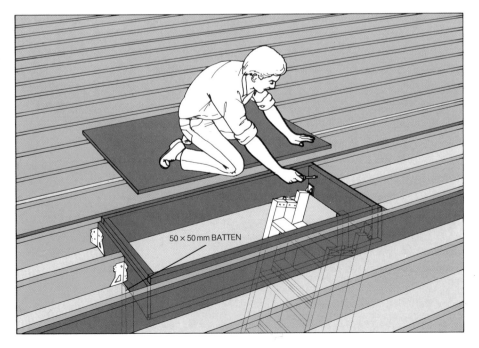

50 × 50 mm BATTEN

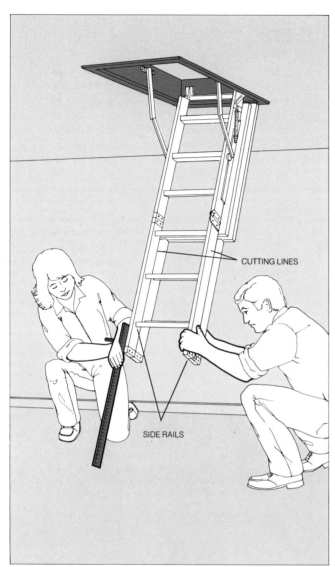

CUTTING LINES

SIDE RAILS

2 **Cutting the side rails to size.** Unfold the middle section of the ladder and, following the angle of the ladder, measure the distances from the front and rear edges of this section to the floor. Mark the side rails of the bottom section with these measurements—be careful not to reverse the distances—and draw cutting lines between the marks. Saw along the lines on each side rail and smooth the cuts with a plane.

A Staircase with a Twist

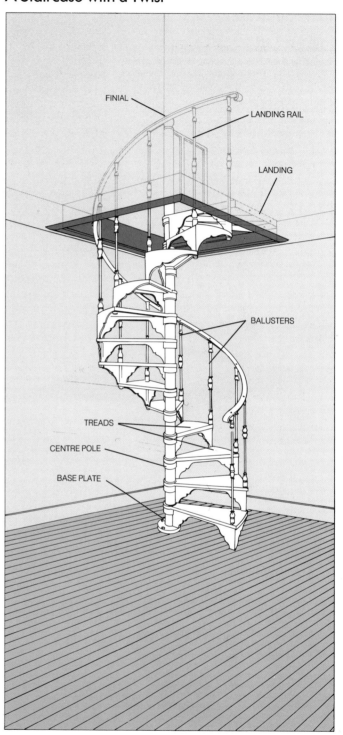

FINIAL

LANDING RAIL

LANDING

BALUSTERS

TREADS

CENTRE POLE

BASE PLATE

Anatomy of a spiral stair. This typical metal staircase which comes in a kit consists of a centre pole mounted on a base plate and 12 treads secured to the pole and braced at their outer edges by balusters. A curving handrail links the balusters; a landing and a landing rail top the stairs. The pole is finished with a decorative capping called a finial.

Assembling and Installing a Spiral Staircase

1 **Positioning the centre pole.** Stretch two strings diagonally from nails driven into opposite corners of the well hole. Drop a plumb line from the intersection of the strings to the floor below and get a helper to mark the spot where the plumb bob touches the floor.

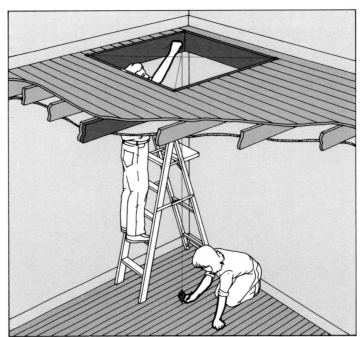

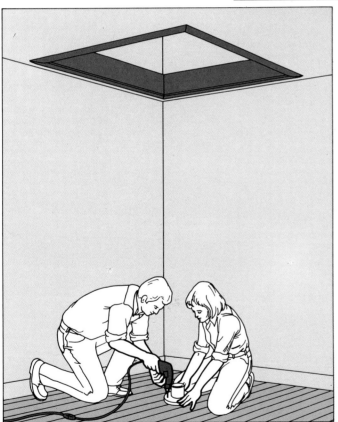

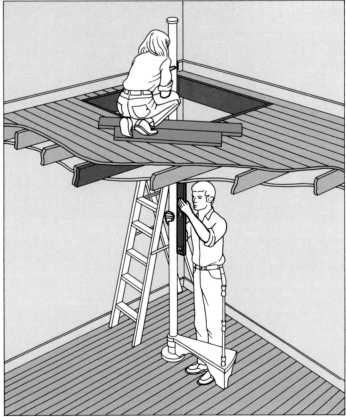

2 **Securing the base plate.** Centre the base plate on the floor mark. While a helper holds the base plate firmly in position, drill pilot holes in the floor through the pre-drilled holes in the plate. Screw the base plate to the floor using the coach screws provided with the kit. On a concrete floor, drill the holes with a masonry bit and secure the plate to the floor with expansion bolts.

3 **Installing the pole.** Refer to the manufacturer's chart to calculate the correct position on the floor for the first tread, then slot the tread with its pre-attached baluster over the base plate. With the aid of your helper, slide the centre pole through the first tread and into the base plate. Check that the pole is vertical using a spirit level.

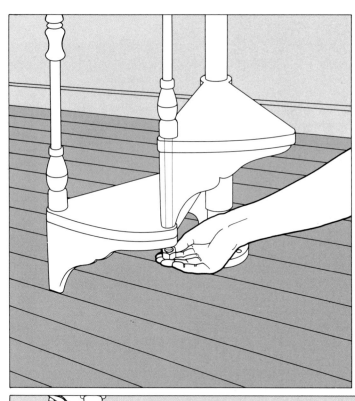

4 **Fitting the treads.** While your helper assists from above, slide the second tread down the pole and position it against the locating lug on the first tread. Slot the second baluster through both the second and first treads, then screw the baluster nut finger tight underneath the first tread. Fit remaining treads and balusters the same way.

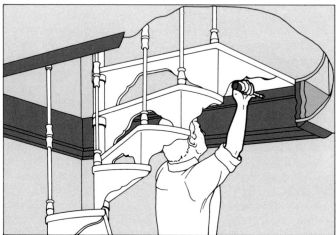

5 **Fixing the landing.** When all the treads and balusters are in position, slide the landing on to the centre pole. Test the staircase for plumb and check that the landing is flush with the upper floor, then fix the landing to the sides of the well hole using the screws supplied *(above)*. Secure the landing rail to the landing, again using the screws supplied.

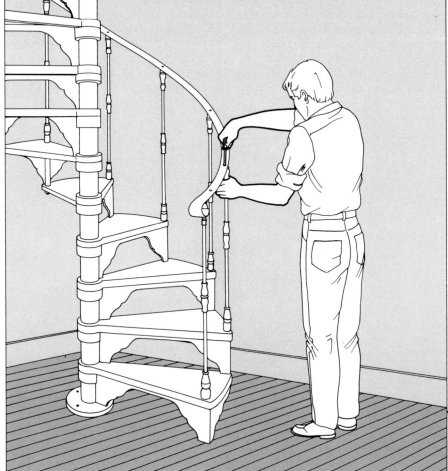

6 **Installing the handrail.** Position the handrail so that the screw holes rest on top of the balusters, then screw the handrail to the baluster heads with the screws supplied *(left)*. Starting at the bottom of the staircase, tighten the baluster nuts under the treads with an adjustable spanner. Finally mount the finial on top of the pole.

Building a Simple Staircase Step by Step

Ancient builders knew the secret of staircase construction thousands of years ago: for comfortable ascent or descent, a precise ratio must be maintained between the distance a person moves forwards and the distance he raises or lowers himself. Today, builders think in terms of "rise" and "going" to calculate the ratio. Rise is the vertical distance between the tops of consecutive treads; going is the horizontal distance between the front edges of treads.

For all domestic stairways—from the simple stairs described here to the finished main staircase shown on pages 90–93— building regulations stipulate that the height of a rise must not exceed 220 mm, while the minimum distance for a going is set at 220 mm. Since stairs should not be as steep as ladders or as shallow as ramps, the "pitch", or angle, of a household staircase must not exceed 42 degrees. As a general rule, for a comfortable pitch the sum of the going plus twice the rise will fall between 600 and 650 mm.

The width of a flight of stairs is also governed by building regulations: 600 mm is permitted in some circumstances, but 800 mm is usually the rule. In addition, there must be a minimum of 2 metres between the nosing of a tread and the ceiling above. When planning the opening for a stairway (pages 78–81), draw the outline of treads and risers on the wall adjacent to the proposed flight. Measure up to the ceiling from the nose of each tread, marking for your opening only where this distance is more than 2 metres.

To determine the crucial measurements for the staircase, first decide on a convenient rise (generally between 175 and 200 mm) and divide this figure into the total rise—the distance between the upper and lower floors. Round fractions up for a shallower stair or down for a steeper one, then divide this figure into the total rise and round off the result to give the height of a single rise. Decide on a convenient going and multiply this figure by the number of rises minus one for the total going.

Marking the strings with the exact locations of the treads and rises is best done with a pitchboard, a right-angled triangle of plywood marked with the going and rise dimensions (below). Bear in mind that strings are what builders call "handed"— the measured-up sides face inwards and must therefore be marked, not identically but in a mirror-image of each other.

Housing for treads can be cut with hand tools, but an electric router will speed up this time-consuming job. A plywood template guides the cutting edge of the router round an area exactly equal to the dimensions of the tread ends. Before starting work, practise using the router by making several trial cuts on scrap timber.

Risers are not structurally necessary in a staircase of this type. For safety's sake, however, building regulations prohibit an opening of more than 100 mm between treads. The design here calls for semi-risers glued and nailed underneath each tread. These satisfy legal requirements, while demanding no special housing or complicated fitting techniques.

Treads can be cut from any timber; they should be at least 32 mm thick for stairs 600 mm wide and 38 mm thick for stairs 800 mm wide. The strings must be wide enough to provide a margin of at least 50 mm both above and below the stairs— boards 225 to 275 mm are generally large enough. Use timber 32 to 50 mm thick for both the strings.

Finally, no staircase is complete without a handrail. The simple one described here is sturdy and easy to install; see pages 74–77 for building regulations relating to handrails and instructions on installing a more sophisticated balustrade.

1 Making the pitchboard. Mark the length of the going and the height of the rise along adjacent edges of a square-cornered piece of 6 mm plywood. Draw a line—the margin line—between the marks, then draw a second, parallel line 50 mm from the first. Align a batten with the second line and pin it to the plywood; then pin a second batten to the opposite side (right). Saw off the plywood behind the battens.

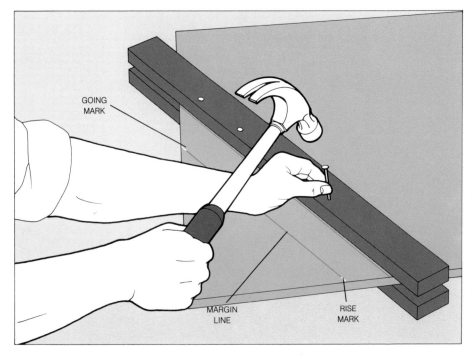

GOING MARK

MARGIN LINE

RISE MARK

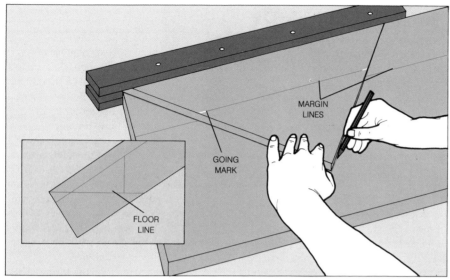

2 Marking the bottom of the string. Draw a margin line 50 mm in from the long edge of one of the strings. Set the pitchboard at one end of the string with its going side facing the end. The margin line should be aligned with that on the string. Mark the string along the going side of the pitchboard, then along the rise side to the edge of the board *(left)*. Using a straightedge, extend the going line to the opposite edges of the string to form the floor line *(inset)*.

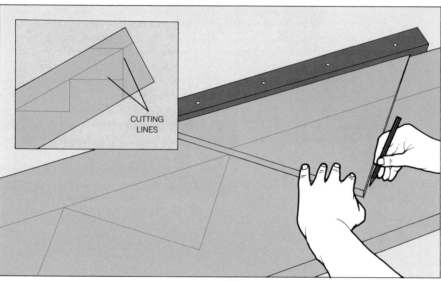

3 Marking for the treads and rises. Mark the remaining treads and rises by sliding the pitchboard along the string and marking along its going side and rise side as far as the margin line *(left)*. Extend the final rise line to the bottom of the string, then mark across the top edge of the string at right angles to the top of this rise line *(inset)*. Cut off the top of the string along these two lines; cut off the bottom of the string along the floor line and the first rise line. Cut a 100 by 50 mm notch in the bottom of the string for the kick plate *(page 89, Step 9)*. Mark and cut the second string in the same way.

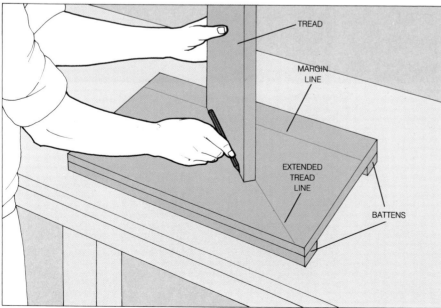

4 Making a housing template. Pin two 50 by 25 mm battens to a 600 by 350 mm rectangle of 12 mm plywood so that they are parallel with the long sides, and the width of the string apart. Place this framework—the housing template—over one string and mark a margin line across its surface. Remove the battens from the pitchboard and place it on the template with the margin lines aligned; trace along the going side of the pitchboard, then extend this tread line to the edges of the template. Remove the pitchboard and also the template from the string. Stand a tread on the template below the tread line, and trace its outline *(left)*. Enlarge the tread outline all round by a distance equal to the gap between the cutter and the circular collar on your router.

5 Routing the string. Using a keyhole saw, make an opening in the housing template by cutting round the enlarged tread outline. Support one of the strings on sawhorses, then place the template over the string at one end. Align the first tread line on the string with the tread line on the template, and pin the template temporarily to the string. Rout out the housing to a depth of 14 mm in two cuts, each 7 mm deep. Repeat this operation for each tread line on both strings; housings for the first and last treads will reach the sawn-off ends of the strings. Finally, square off the corners of the housings with a chisel.

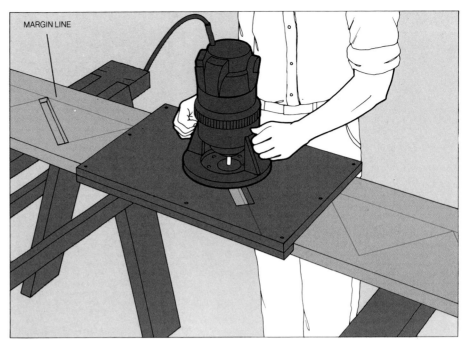

MARGIN LINE

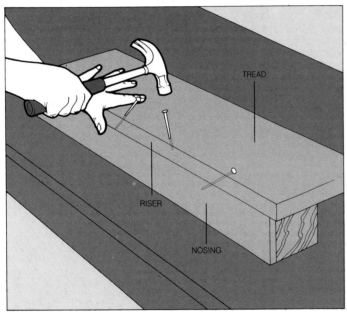

TREAD

RISER

NOSING

6 Preparing the treads and risers. Cut treads exactly 28 mm longer than the planned width of your stairs, and cut risers to the width of the stairs from lengths of 75 by 25 mm timber. With the risers set back 25 mm from the nosings of the treads, support each tread-and-riser unit on a block of wood and secure the riser to the tread with PVA adhesive and four 50 mm lost-head nails which should be driven down through the tread in dovetailed pairs (above).

Drill two pilot holes to take No. 12 screws through each housing in both strings. With a helper, test the fit of each tread and riser unit by tapping the treads into the housings of one string and fitting the second string on top. Chamfer round the tread ends with a plane, where necessary, to secure a perfect fit, then number the treads and remove them from the strings.

7 Assembling the stairs. Put the bottom tread and riser aside and, keeping to the same order as in the dry run, glue all the others into the housings of one string, using PVA adhesive. Apply adhesive to the exposed tread ends. Then, with your helper gradually lowering one end of the second string, fit the housings over the treads, one by one, until the string is in position. Make sure the fit is secure by tapping along the length of the string with a mallet and block of wood (above). Use a square to check that the treads are at right angles to the strings; adjust, if necessary, by moving the second string slightly. Then drive 50 mm No. 12 screws through the pilot holes in the second string. Carefully turn the staircase over and secure the first string in the same way.

8 **Installing the stairs.** Lift the stairs into position; check that the tops of the strings are level and nail them in place against the trimmer. Then secure the tops with framing connectors, bending the end of one leg of each connector to fit the bottom of the trimmer *(inset)*. Drill three equally spaced pilot holes along the wall string and fix the string to the wall with 63 mm No. 10 screws.

FRAMING CONNECTOR

9 **Fastening strings to the floor.** For a concrete floor, position a 100 by 50 mm kick plate under the notches in the strings and drill holes through it just far enough to mark the concrete. Then set it aside and use a masonry bit to drill holes for plugs. Replace the plate, fasten it to the floor with 75 mm No. 10 screws and plugs and toenail the strings to it. Tap the lower tread into its housing, securing it with PVA adhesive and screws through the outer string.

For a timber floor, where a kick plate is not necessary, use a framing connector to fasten the strings to the floor.

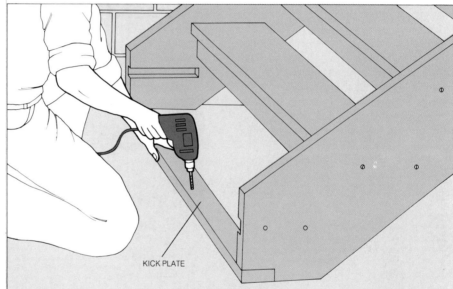

KICK PLATE

10 **Installing a simple handrail.** Cut two newel posts from lengths of 100 by 75 mm timber. Clamp them in position to the outside of the outer string—one at the top of the stairs and one at the bottom—then check that they are vertical and secure each with two 10 mm coach bolts. Bolt a third post, cut from 100 by 50 mm timber, to the centre of the flight. Using 150 by 37 mm timber, make three rails to run the length of the stairs; round off the top of the handrail with a plane. Space the rails evenly and fasten them to the inside of the posts with two 50 mm No. 10 screws at each post. The top of the handrail must be between 840 mm and 1 metre above the nosing of the treads. Newel posts should rise at least 50 mm above the handrail; trim the centre post off flush with the rail. Finally, sand down any roughness on the tops and corners of the posts.

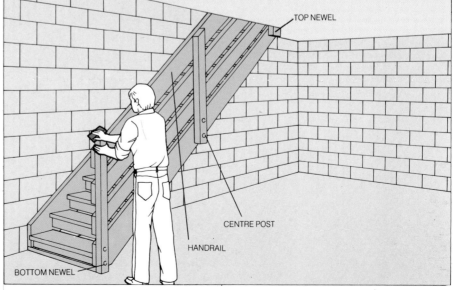

TOP NEWEL

CENTRE POST

HANDRAIL

BOTTOM NEWEL

A Craftsman's Pride: the Prefab Staircase

To replace a main staircase or make an attractive passageway to a newly finished basement or attic, you may want something rather more elaborate than the type of stairs that are shown on the preceding pages. The best solution, both handsome and economical, is a factory-built staircase. You can assemble a graceful balustrade for the staircase yourself, from stock parts.

The stair manufacturer will make a staircase to your own particular specifications and, usually about two to six weeks after you place your order, deliver the finished unit to your home. You must prepare the opening in the upper floor *(pages 78–81)* and then, with helpers, fit the newel posts and handrail and secure the staircase to the opening and the adjoining wall.

Ordering the stairs correctly, of course, is the crucial first step. Some manufacturers have local representatives who will help you to choose a staircase and write the appropriate specifications for it. If you submit your own specifications, you must tell the manufacturer the total rise, total going and width. It is important to bear in mind at all times that whatever you decide upon

has to be in line with the building regulations *(page 86)*.

The manufacturer must also be told whether the stairs will be fully or partially open; any open side must be fitted with a balustrade *(pages 74–77)* and there must be a landing rail along all the unwalled sides of the opening.

As well as the staircase itself, the manufacturer will provide a landing tread, or nosing, for the transition between the top of the stairs and the finish floor. To make good, use an apron lining or, alternatively, you can use sheets of plywood as described on page 93. If you are intending to box in the underside of the stairs *(page 93, bottom)*, ask the manufacturer to rebate the bottom of both strings.

Although the staircase will be assembled in the factory, there are several essential adjustments to make before it can be raised and fixed into position. The landing newel must be notched so as to slot over the combined depth of the trimmer and ceiling at the stair opening. The wall string will need careful measuring and cutting both at the top, where it hooks over the trim-

mer, and at the bottom, where it must rest evenly on the floor.

The newel posts and handrail are also installed while the staircase is still on its side. These will already have been tested for accurate fitting at the factory, but it would nevertheless be wise to have a dry run, checking that all of the mortise and tenon joints fit perfectly before you begin to glue them together.

A staircase is held in place partly by its own weight; the landing nosing is notched securely over the trimmer at the stair opening. For added stability, it is bolted or screwed through the landing newel post to the trimmer, and screwed to the wall through the string. Traditionally, the floor newel post is also fixed in place in one of two ways: either it is bedded in a concrete screed or, as described here, it may be anchored with a steel dowel.

Balusters, whether simple posts or slender spindles of turned wood, give a staircase its individual character. Assemble these by the method described on pages 74–77 when all the other work has been completed.

Installing the Staircase

1 Cutting the top of the wall string. Place the staircase on its side, supporting the wall string across two sawhorses. Slot the top riser and landing nosing into their housings. Then, starting at the lower edge of the wall string, trace a pencil line along the inside of the riser and the nosing *(right)*. From the back of the landing nosing, extend the line upwards to the height of the skirting (generally about 75 mm) and then square off the line across the top corner of the string *(inset)*. Remove the top riser and landing nosing and cut along the pencil line with a handsaw. The string will now match up with both the skirting board and the stairwell trimmer.

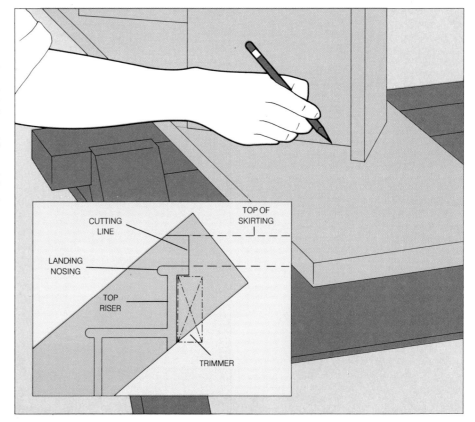

CUTTING LINE

TOP OF SKIRTING

LANDING NOSING

TOP RISER

TRIMMER

2 **Cutting the bottom of the wall string.** The floor line may already have been marked on the wall string by the manufacturer. If not, mark the line yourself, drawing it parallel to the bottom tread. If you intend to lay a finish floor after installing the staircase, move the floor line down the string by the thickness of the finish floor. Saw off the bottom of the string along the floor line. Then set a combination square to the height of the skirting and slide it along the cut edge of the string until the measured leg of the square intersects the top edge of the string. Draw a perpendicular line up from the base of the string at this point *(right)* and cut along it, squaring off the string to the height of the adjacent skirting.

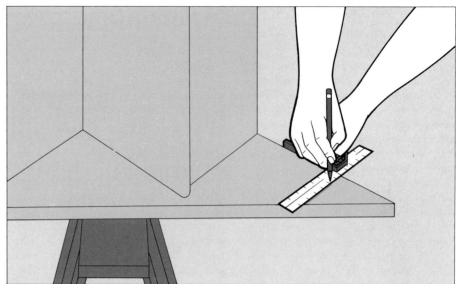

3 **Marking and cutting the top newel post.** Place the top newel post on a work bench, the housed side uppermost. Using a combination square, extend the line formed by the top of the housing round the back of the post and across the opposite side. Measure down from this line the distance between the finish floor at the stair opening and the surface of the ceiling below, then draw a second line round the back and opposite sides of the post, parallel with the first *(right)*. Now place the top riser in its housing; trace a line along its back edge and extend this between the first two lines. Draw a matching line on the opposite side of the post. Shade in the area defined by the four lines *(inset)* and cut it out with a saw and a chisel.

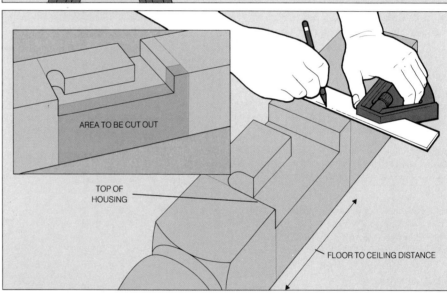

AREA TO BE CUT OUT

TOP OF HOUSING

FLOOR TO CEILING DISTANCE

4 **Installing the newels and handrail.** Turn the staircase over so that the outer string is resting on the sawhorses. Apply PVA adhesive to the twin tenons at the upper end of the string and fit the mortised side of the top newel post on to the string *(right)*. Glue the upper end of the handrail to the newel post; then, while a helper steadies the handrail, glue the lower newel in place, first to the handrail, then to the string.

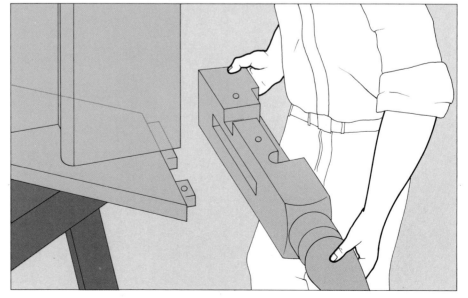

5 Completing the assembly. With a mallet, drive timber dowels into the pre-drilled holes in the newel posts—generally two dowels at the string *(right)* and one dowel at the handrail. If the lower newel is not cut to length, saw it off level with the floor line. Then glue the top riser and landing nosing into their housings in the strings, wiping off excess glue with a damp cloth. Wait an hour or so for the glue to dry before proceeding.

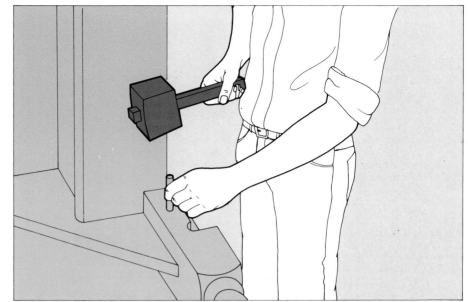

6 Positioning the staircase. With the help of at least two assistants, one stationed on the upper floor, raise the staircase temporarily into position. Hook the landing nosing and the recessed newel post over the trimmer at the stair opening. Check a tread for level, both side to side and front to back, and adjust as necessary with scraps of plywood or hardboard under the bottom of the wall string or newel post. Trace the outline of the newel post base on the floor *(right)*.

Lower the staircase and rest it again on the sawhorses. Drill a 12 mm hole, 50 mm deep, into the centre of the base of the lower newel post. In the centre of the pencilled outline on the floor, drill a second 12 mm hole—50 mm deep for a concrete floor, through the floorboards for a timber floor. Insert a 12 mm steel dowel in the base of the newel. Lift the staircase back into position, pushing the dowel into the hole drilled in the floor *(inset)*.

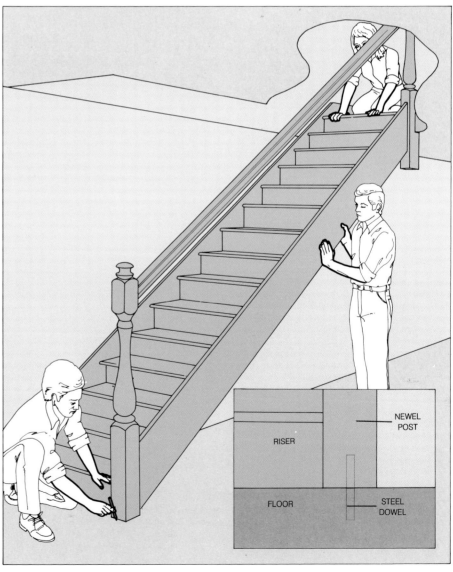

RISER

NEWEL POST

FLOOR

STEEL DOWEL

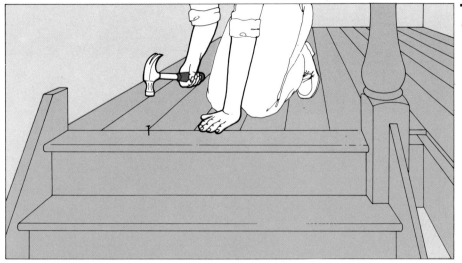

7 Securing the staircase. With the staircase in position and the treads level, drive two 50 mm lost-head nails through the landing nosing and into the trimmer *(left)*. Then fix the wall string to the wall with three 63 mm No. 10 screws, evenly spaced along the length of the stairs. If there is no ceiling in place, secure the landing newel post to the trimmer with two 12 mm coach bolts. Where a ceiling prevents access to the back of the trimmer, drive two 87 mm No. 10 screws into the trimmer from the stair side of the string, inserting them through holes pre-drilled in the newel.

Some Finishing Touches

Making good round the stair opening. Line the edges of the floor above your stairs with strips of 75 by 22 mm nosing, cut so as to butt against the floorboards and overlap the stair opening. Nail them down to trimmers and trimmer joints. Clad the inside of the opening with an "apron" of 12 mm plywood, held in place with 37 mm oval nails *(left)*. Where a ceiling has been cut away, cover the under-surfaces of trimmers and trimming joists with 9 mm plasterboard. Conceal the joint between apron and ceiling with 12 mm quadrant moulding.

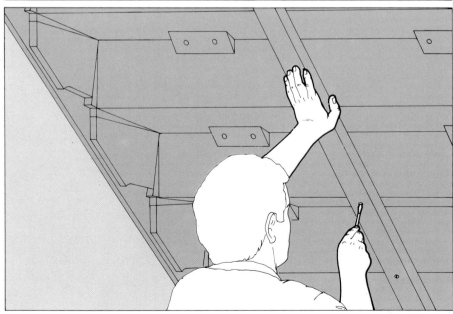

Boxing in under the stairs. Fix 50 by 25 mm battens up the centre of the understairs, securing them end to end with 37 mm No. 8 screws driven up into the treads. Cut sheets of plasterboard to fit across the width of the stairs and slot the sides of the plasterboard into the rebated edges of the strings. Fix the plasterboard to the central batten and the strings with plasterboard nails at 150 mm centres. Conceal the joint between the plasterboard and the strings with mouldings.

Carpets for Warmth and Softness

Tightening a hessian-backed carpet. The metal knee-kicker in the centre forces carpet on to spiked gripper bars installed alongside the skirting boards of a room. Everywhere else in the room, the carpet rests upon the lightly textured side of a sheet of underlay; the rough waffled side of the underlay *(top, right)* should face the floor.

Wall-to-wall carpeting, once a luxury reserved for the rich, is available to everyone now. Synthetic materials have made it so easy and inexpensive to install that it has become the flooring of choice in many new homes and flats. And with good reason. Carpeting is safe and warm, soft and colourful. It soaks up sound. It camouflages defects in a floor and it can be laid over almost any surface without special preparation. Maintenance is simple: cleaning is a matter of regular vacuuming and occasional shampooing; stains can be removed with common cleaning agents; and most kinds of damage can be repaired at home.

As a decorative element, carpet is the most versatile of floorings. It works well in any room, even a kitchen or a bathroom, and comes in a variety of fibres. Wool, the oldest of all, is warm, handsome and springy to walk on; it retains its good looks well and shows soiling less than other fibres. Among the synthetics, the best acrylic carpets look and handle like wool but require frequent cleaning. Nylon tends to flatten quickly and soils easily unless specially treated; it is often used in blends to give extra durability. The economy fibre is rayon; it is often blended with other fibres to add bulk, but by itself is neither resilient nor easy to clean. Polypropylene flattens easily but is resistant to moisture and very hard-wearing. Blends of different materials offer the combined characteristics of the constituent fibres.

Along with synthetic fibres have come new manufacturing techniques. At one time, all carpets were woven on looms, like fine tapestry. Today, the great majority are tufted, made by machines that sew pile yarn into a backing fabric. The machines produce carpet many times faster than the largest looms, at a fraction of the cost.

Because wool and woven carpets are so expensive, the charge for professional installation is a relatively minor part of their total cost. The tufted synthetics, however, are particularly suited to amateur installation, especially the foam-backed variety that can be secured directly to the floor with double-sided adhesive tape. Hessian-backed carpets require a separate underlay and a slightly more complex installation, but labour-saving devices make the job easier. A knee-kicker, for example, will stretch the carpet smooth and taut, and gripper bars—plywood battens bristled with projecting spikes—invisibly hold a carpet to the floor, eliminating the visible tacks once used for fastening. These tools and materials mean that the traditional carpet craftsman, with a mouthful of tacks and a handful of needles and thread, is now a figure of the past. With reasonable care and clear instructions, you can do the job yourself.

Estimating and Installing Wall-to-Wall Carpet

Carpet-laying was once an arcane art performed by veteran craftsmen who invisibly stitched together the seams and deftly placed hundreds of tacks to carpet even a small room. Nowadays, however, changes in the carpet-manufacturing process have so simplified the job that it can be done by an amateur.

There are two commonly available types of carpet: foam backed, which has a layer of foam padding bonded to its back, and hessian backed, which must be laid over a separate underlay. Foam-backed carpets are very much simpler to lay (pages 98–104). Hessian-backed carpets, on the other hand, will usually be more hard-wearing, but their installation requires the use of special tools and the more complicated fitting techniques which are described on pages 105–109.

Some carpets are still made in the traditional way: the pile—that is, the fibres that constitute the cushiony surface—is woven directly into a backing of tough, open-weave jute-and-cotton threads that give a carpet its horizontal strength. Such carpets as Axminster or Wilton require special installation techniques that are best left to professionals. These kinds of carpets are so expensive that the cost of having them professionally installed—charged per square metre, regardless of the price of the carpet—is a proportionately small additional expense.

Most carpets are tufted: that is, their pile—whether made of wool or any of a number of synthetics—is machine-stitched into a backing that is made beforehand. They may be made with loop pile or cut pile (right, below), a distinction that is important as it determines the techniques to be used when cutting carpet to fit your room (page 98). Sculptured carpets are made with both loop and cut pile.

In all carpets, the "pile direction"—the direction in which the fibres are pressed when a newly manufactured carpet is rolled up after coming off the machines—will affect the appearance and the installation technique. You can tell pile direction by stroking it: stroking against the pile will raise the nap. When you "look into" the pile of a carpet, with the fibres leaning towards you, the carpet takes on its deepest hue. When you are "looking over" the pile—that is, with the fibres leaning away from you—the carpet will appear flatter and lighter in colour.

Most suppliers offer a free measuring and estimating service, which you should take advantage of, if possible, so that you can calculate more easily how much carpet you will need. Failing this, the best approach is to draw a scale plan on graph paper. Draw the outline of the room first, ignoring any items of built-in furniture, and then mark in the doors and windows—these features will affect the final arrangement of the carpet sections.

Cut strips scaled to the carpet width from another sheet of graph paper, and mark each strip with an arrow to indicate the pile direction. Then arrange the strips on your scale plan of the room, bearing in mind the following points:

☐ The pile direction of the carpet strips must always run the same way, regardless of seams. If possible, the pile should lean towards the main entrance of the room, so that the carpet presents its fullest, richest appearance. To avoid the problem of shading, the pile should run away from the room's main source of natural light.

☐ Never run a seam into a doorway, where it could be loosened or distorted by heavy foot traffic. Try to position seams at right angles to a window or so that they will be covered by furniture.

☐ On patterned carpets, you must take into account the "pattern match"—the distance from the point where a pattern begins to where it begins again—in order to be sure of matching the pattern along a seam. If your scheme involves matching the pattern only lengthways across two original edges of the carpet (opposite page), simply allow for a full extra pattern match on one of the lengths. You will be able to adjust the strips when you are actually installing the carpet.

When the strips representing carpet widths have been positioned on the plan to your satisfaction, add up the lengths of each full width, allowing an extra 150 to 200 mm on each. You may find that you are able to cut two or three filler pieces from each full width of carpet, but otherwise ignore any wastage from cutting. Take your estimates and plan along to the supplier and ask him to double-check your calculations before cutting the carpet.

Use the same scale plan to work out how much adhesive tape or underlay and gripper (page 105) will be required. Measure round the perimeter of the plan to estimate for the tape or gripper, and buy a metre or so extra to allow for any possible mistakes. For underlay, calculate the area of the room in square metres and add on a little more to cover wastage.

Before starting to lay a carpet, remove any doors opening into the room and any quadrant moulding running along the bottom of the skirting boards. Nail or screw down loose boards in a timber floor, punch any protruding nail heads and fill cracks with wood strips or a paste of sawdust and floor finish (page 8); if necessary, install a hardboard underlayment (page 46) in order to provide a smooth, level base for the carpet. Vacuum the floor thoroughly. Level an uneven concrete floor with a self-levelling compound and, if the surface of the concrete is dusty, prime it with a proprietary sealant.

Rehang inward-opening doors after the carpet has been installed. If the carpet pile catches against the door, making it difficult to open or close, plane the bottom of the door with a block plane or alternatively install rising-butt hinges that lift the door above the carpet as it opens.

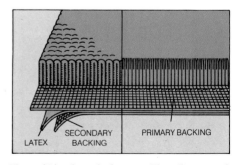

The making of a tufted carpet. The pile yarn of tufted carpet is stitched through a layer of open-weave fabric, the primary backing. A second fabric backing is stuck under the first, usually with a coating of latex. When the yarn is left uncut the result is loop-pile tufted carpet (above, left). But the tops of the loops are often split or cut off, making cut-pile tufted carpet (above, right).

Fitting Carpet to the Room

Lengthways installation. In this room, 5.8 by 6.8 metres, the best plan is lengthways installation of broadloom 4 metres wide; the rest is filled with two pieces *(1 and 2)* from an extra 4 metres of carpet *(dashed lines, far right)*. The major seam will run into the main light source—the window on the left. The pile should lean towards the main door. The large section of full-width carpet will take most of the room's traffic, which passes between the two doors. The seams will be away from heavy traffic and probably partly hidden by furniture. In a smaller room, fill the gap between the main run of carpet and the wall at the top of the drawing with sections so narrow you can cut three or more from the 4 metre broadloom width; if you do this, you will have to make more seams, but will be paying for less carpet.

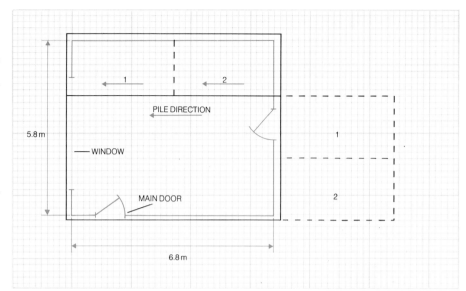

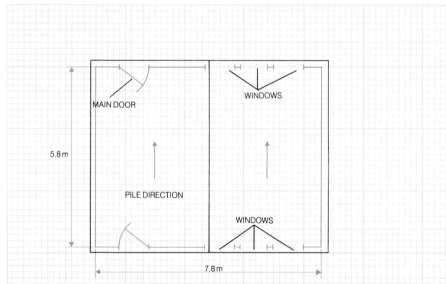

Short sheeting a room. This room, measuring 5.8 by 7.8 metres, has an arrangement of doors and windows that makes it preferable to install the length of the carpet across the shorter dimension of the room—a technique called short sheeting. That way, the major seam will be aligned with the light from the windows and will be away from the bulk of traffic that passes between the doors. The pile of the carpet should lean towards the main door.

If either of the doors were at the centre of the wall, the above arrangement would mean that the seam ran straight into it, taking the wear of heavy traffic. In this situation, one of the full widths of carpet should be cut lengthways into two pieces and then seamed to both sides of the remaining full width section, which would thus straddle the door.

The Right Carpet for the Right Room

Colour, design and fibre *(page 95)* are not the only factors that should determine your choice of carpet. For all types of carpet, the following factors should also be taken into consideration.

☐ WEARABILITY. Carpets are graded according to their wearability and most suppliers specify the appropriate usage and expected carpet life on their display rolls. As a general rule, choose a heavy-wear hessian-backed carpet for hallways and staircases; playrooms and bedrooms will require a general or medium-wear carpet; and infrequently used rooms such as spare bedrooms or a dining room can be carpeted in a medium or light-wear

grade. If you are worried about the possibility of the carpet becoming soiled, choose one that has been treated to resist stains. Some carpets which are specially designed for use in bathrooms are machine washable.

☐ TEXTURE. Shag pile needs regular combing with a carpet rake; it is not suitable for stairs or rooms with heavy traffic but adds a note of luxury to a bedroom. Twisted pile, in which the yarn is twisted so that each tuft lies at an angle to its neighbour, is better than straight-cut pile for avoiding footmarks and shading. Loop pile has similar wearing characteristics but is more difficult to clean

thoroughly than cut pile. With all types of texture, choose a carpet with a dense pile—the closer together the tufts, the more hard-wearing the carpet will be. The depth of pile and the weight of the carpet are not by themselves indications of good quality.

☐ SIZE. For most rooms, choose a wide carpet roll that will require the minimum number of seams. Broadloom carpet (this term describes carpet woven on a wide loom) is usually either 3.69 or 4 metres wide. But for landings and hall passages, body or strip carpet—which comes in narrow widths of 690 to 910 mm—may prove to be more economical.

Laying a Foam-Backed Carpet

The simplest and cleanest way of securing foam-backed carpet to the floor is to stick double-sided adhesive tape at least 50 mm wide round the perimeter of the room. The traditional alternative—that of applying adhesive across the whole surface of the floor—is now used mostly for commercial premises, where the carpet must withstand continuous wear and the movement of heavy furniture. A third option, laying the carpet loose on the floor, is practical only for small rooms in which the carpet is unlikely to be disturbed by heavy traffic.

Both the tape and the binder bars for protecting the edges of the carpet at doorways can be purchased from your carpet dealer. Binder bars for doorways between a carpet and a hard floor surface such as ceramic tile have an integral flange that is pressed down on to the carpet edge; for doorways between two carpeted rooms, choose a binder bar with a separate capping strip that is fitted on to the bar after the carpet has been installed.

Before cutting the carpet, unroll it in an empty room—or outside the house on a layer of newspaper—and give it time to flatten. Then, referring back to the scale plan which you made, carefully measure, mark and cut the carpet to the lengths required, allowing an extra 75 mm round each piece for trimming later. Loop-pile carpet is cut from the front (pile side up) to ensure that it is cut through the loops; all other carpets are cut from the back (*opposite page, below*).

The separate carpet sections are then re-rolled and brought into the room for laying out, beginning with the longest section that goes alongside a wall. When the floor has been completely covered, the carpet is rolled back to allow the underlay to be positioned and secured (*page 100*); because paper felt underlay is so light, it could very easily tear or move out of line if it were laid before the carpet.

The carpet should then be trodden out to ensure that it lies completely flat, and left to settle for about a week. To fit the carpet, relief cuts are made at corners and round other obstacles, and the seams between adjacent sections are cut and secured (*pages 101–103*). The installation process is completed by trimming the carpet to the wall edges, fixing it to the double-sided adhesive tape, and securing the flanges or attaching the capping strips of the binder bars (*page 104*).

Preparing the Floor

Securing double-sided tape. Starting in one corner of the room, unroll the doubled-sided tape and press it firmly to the floor about 7 mm from the wall along the length of the room. Cut the tape at the end of the wall, then repeat this procedure along the remaining walls until the whole perimeter of the room is taped. Stick down and cut short sections of tape as necessary to negotiate bays and built-in furniture. Do not remove the protective backing on the top side of the tape.

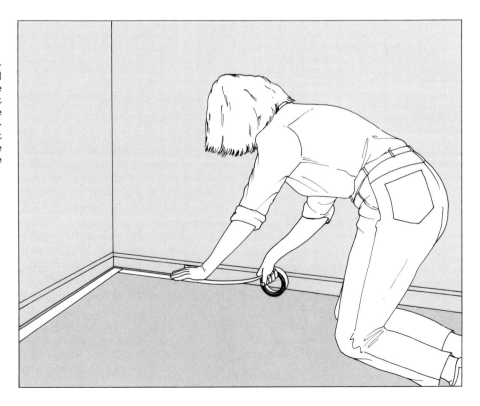

Installing binder bars in doorways. Position the binder bar so that the metal flange that will cover the carpet edge lies directly under the door when closed. Depending on the width and design of the binder bar, you may have to notch the ends with a hacksaw to accommodate the doorstops or rebates on the frame jambs. Secure the binder bar by driving nails or screws through the pre-drilled holes; on tiled floors, use a cement-based adhesive. On binder bars with an integral flange *(right)*, leave the flange open until the carpet has been laid.

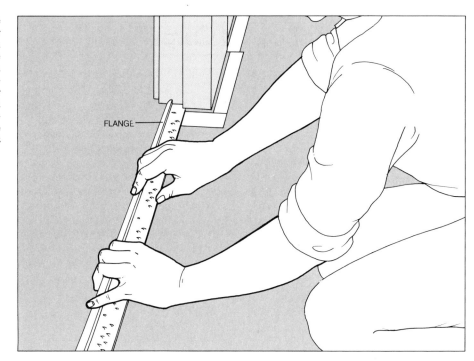

FLANGE

Rough-Cutting the Carpet

Cutting a straight line. Measure the required length along both edges of the carpet, allowing an extra 150 mm for trimming, and cut notches on both sides. For a cut-pile carpet *(right)*, fold the carpet back and snap a chalk line across the backing between the notches. Cut along the chalked line with a trimming knife, using a metal straightedge to guide the blade. The blade should be extended just enough to cut through the backing; to protect the face of the carpet underneath the section being cut, you can place a timber board between the two layers.

For a loop-pile carpet *(inset)*, snap a string across the face of the carpet between the notches and mark the cutting line on the pile using tailor's chalk and a metal straightedge. Remove the string from the carpet and cut along the line with scissors or shears.

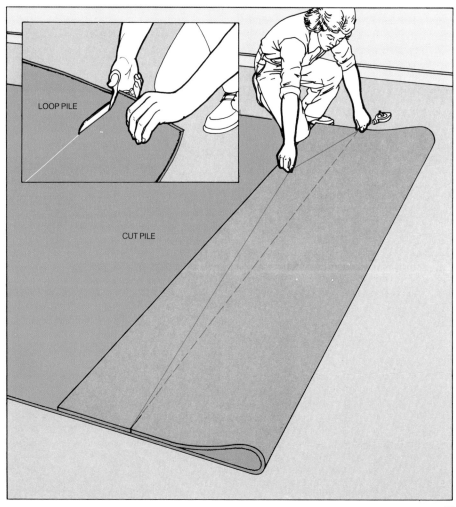

LOOP PILE

CUT PILE

Positioning the Carpet and Underlay

Kicking carpet into place. Unroll each section of carpet in its planned position on the floor, lapping the edges of the carpet up the wall by about 75 mm. To manoeuvre each section into its correct position, straddle it and kick the carpet with your foot *(right)*. Caution: do not kick the carpet with your heel, as it may tear.

Laying paper felt underlay. Pull back one end of the carpet half way across the room, folding each corner over like an envelope flap *(below, left)*. Then roll out the first sheet of paper felt so that it lies flat on the floor between the carpet and the wall, with its edges about 25 mm away from the double-sided adhesive tape. Overlap the edge of the next sheet on to the first by about 10 mm *(below, right)*. When you have covered the exposed half of the floor, unfold the carpet back over the paper felt underlay, taking care not to dislodge the felt. Then repeat the procedure from the other side of the room.

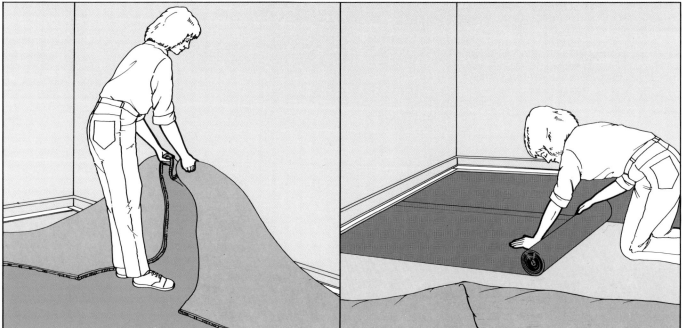

Relief Cuts for Corners and Obstacles

Cutting for external corners. Roll the carpet up to the corner and press it firmly into the angle between the floor and the wall facing you, then fold the excess carpet back. With a trimming knife, make a horizontal cut parallel to the floor and about 50 mm above floor level *(right)*; stop the cut 50 mm short of the corner. Make a diagonal cut from the bottom of the corner to this point *(right, centre)*. Unfold the carpet round the corner and smooth it flat on the floor, then trim off the waste section of carpet about 50 mm above floor level *(right, below)*.

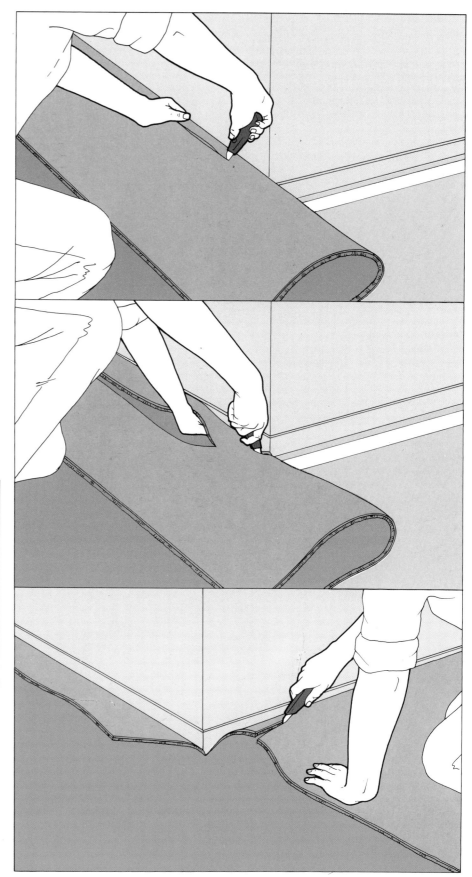

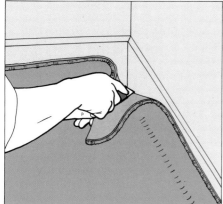

Cutting for an internal corner. Press the carpet firmly into the corner, using a metal rule to force it down into the angles between the floor and the wall. Holding the carpet in place with one hand, fold back the overlap and use a trimming knife to make a vertical relief cut from the bottom of the corner to the edge of the overlap. The carpet can then be smoothed flat to fit snugly into the corner before trimming. Do not extend the cut beyond the section of carpet that will be trimmed off.

Cutting for pipes and radiators. Lap the carpet up against the obstacle, fold it back and make a straight cut from there to the carpet's edge; then make a crosscut just long enough for the carpet to lie roughly flat around the obstacle until you get to final trimming. For a radiator this may involve several cuts out to the edge and several crosscuts to accommodate all the feet and pipes. To make a neat finish, the crosscut edges of the carpet can be folded under instead of trimmed off.

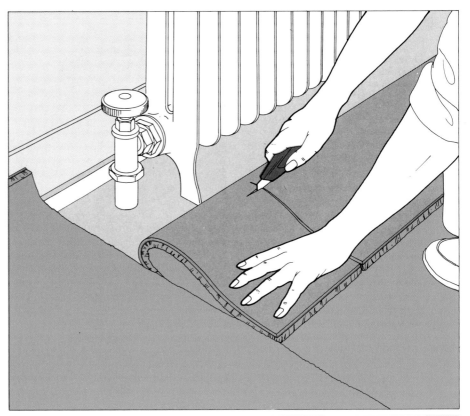

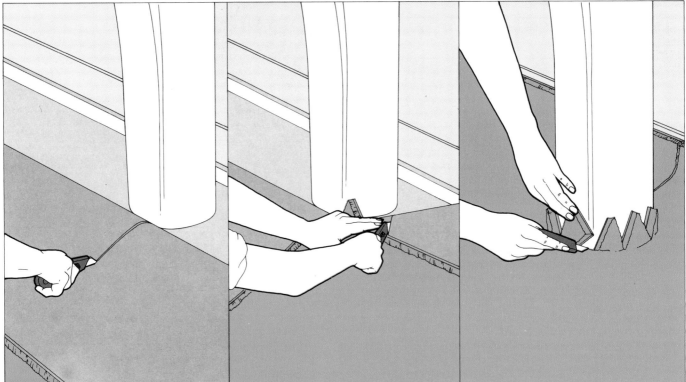

Cutting for a W.C. or basin pedestal. Roll the carpet up to the base of the pedestal, press it down into the angle, then fold it back and make a straight cut from the centre point of the pedestal at floor level to the carpet's edge *(above, left)*. Ease both sides of the carpet round the pedestal, making relief cuts down to the floor on both sides to keep the carpet flat *(above, centre)*. When the cut edges meet at the rear of the pedestal, the carpet around the base will resemble a crown. Press the carpet firmly into the angle between the pedestal base and the floor by running the back of the trimming knife round it; then, holding the blade flat, trim off the crown by cutting into the crease *(above, right)*. Tuck any loose tufts down with a screwdriver. Secure the join between the cut edges at the rear of the pedestal with double-sided tape, as for a seam *(opposite page)*.

Making the Seams

1 Cutting the edges. For seams between carpet sections, overlap the edges by at least 50 mm, then press the blade of a trimming knife through both layers of carpet at several points along the intended line of the seam *(right)*. Fold back one piece of carpet; use a metal straightedge and marker pen to mark a line connecting all the cuts, then trim the carpet along the marked line. Repeat for the second piece of carpet, then press both the cut edges on to the floor to check that they match exactly.

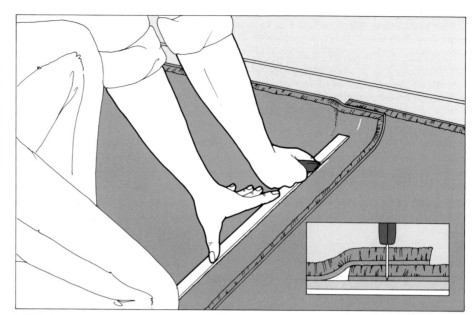

2 Sticking down the tape. Fold back one piece of carpet and hold it down with a weight. Mark the floor along the edge of the second piece, then fold back and weight the second piece also. Press double-sided adhesive tape on to the floor, centred along the marked line *(right)*, then peel off the protective backing on the top side of the tape. Roll one piece of carpet towards and on to the tape, smoothing the last 25 mm towards the seam. Caution: once the carpet makes contact with the tape it cannot be moved without damaging the backing. If you make a mistake, do not try to pull the carpet up—take up the tape from the floor instead, still attached to the carpet, trim it along the carpet edge and start again with new tape.

3 Completing the seam. Roll the second piece of carpet towards the seam and hold it in position above the tape. Curling the edge in slightly, match up the two backings; then press the carpet down and on to the tape, working from the centre of the seam backwards. Smooth the seam as you work, and trim off any loose tufts with scissors.

If the carpet frays along the cut, apply a thin bead of carpet adhesive to the edge of the backing before you position both pieces over the tape. Take care not to smear adhesive on to the carpet pile; any adhesive that does get on to the pile must be cleaned off immediately with carbon tetrachloride and a white absorbent cloth.

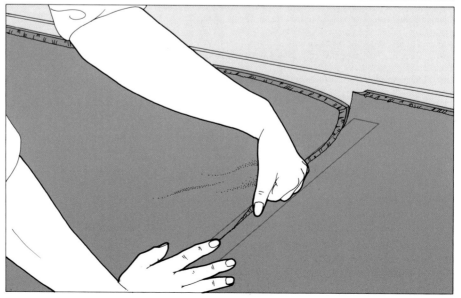

Finishing the Edges

1 **Trimming the carpet.** Force the overlapping carpet edges down into the angle between the wall and the floor with the back of a trimming knife. Check that the blade of the trimming knife is sharp; then, pressing firmly down on a straightedge and holding the knife with its blade at a 45-degree angle to the floor, trim off the overlap by cutting into the crease (*right*).

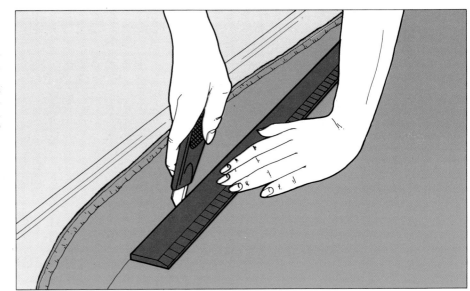

2 **Securing the carpet to the floor.** Starting along the longest wall in the room, fold the carpet back so that it clears the double-sided adhesive tape and weight it down. If the edges of the carpet have frayed, apply a thin bead of adhesive along the backing, taking care to avoid the pile. Peel off the protective backing along the top of the tape, then unfold the carpet and smooth the trimmed edges down on to the tape (*right*).

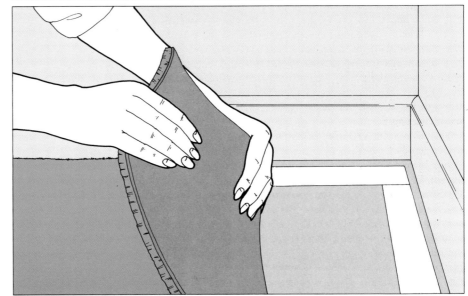

3 **Clamping the carpet at a binder bar.** Trim the carpet to fit under the flange of a binder bar; tuck it in and gently tamp the lip down with a hammer and a block of wood wrapped in a carpet scrap. Bend the lip down a little at a time by moving the block of wood along it after each successive hammer blow.

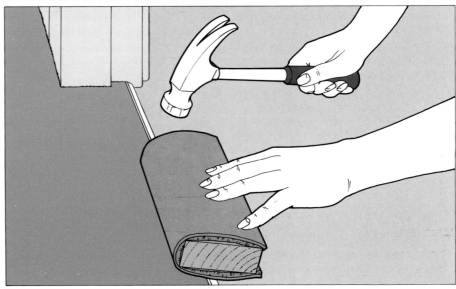

Fitting Woven or Hessian-Backed Carpets

Laid over a cushion of thick underlay, a woven or hessian-backed carpet will last for many years of continuous hard wear. The installation of these carpets, however, involves the use of certain specialized techniques and tools.

To secure the carpet round the perimeter of a room, you will need spiked timber or metal bars known as grippers. The most common form of gripper consists of a slim timber batten with projecting metal spikes on one side (below, right). Grippers are pre-nailed for fixing to the floor; if you are laying carpet over concrete, use grippers with masonry nails.

To choose a gripper with the correct spike length, place a sample of carpet over a gripper and press your fingers into the carpet over the spikes, gingerly at first. The carpet and gripper are ideally matched if you can discern the tips of the spikes without being pricked by them. If you are able to feel the sharpness of the spikes through the carpet, use a gripper which has shorter spikes.

Traditional felt underlay is favoured by professionals because it allows the seams to bed down evenly, but it is now difficult to obtain. The more widely available alternatives are made of rubber; some come with a waffled finish on one side and a paper or sacking-like backing on the other and are usually laid waffle-side down (page 107), but check first against the manufacturer's instructions. On a wooden floor, dust can rise through gaps in the floorboards but a layer of paper felt or ordinary brown paper can be placed beneath the underlay and this will prevent dirt from working its way up through the carpet.

The techniques for laying down the carpet lengths and making the relief cuts for corners and obstacles are the same as for a foam-backed carpet (pages 100–102). The edges for the seams are also cut in the same way, but in place of double-sided adhesive tape—which fixes the carpet to the floor and prevents it from being stretched—use strips of webbing and a latex-based adhesive (page 108, above).

Before final trimming, a hessian-backed carpet must be tightly stretched to make it taut and resistant to creasing. The tool which is used for this job is called a knee-kicker, and can be hired or bought from a carpet trade supplier.

The knee-kicker has an adjustable gripping head on one end, a cushion for the knee on the other, and an adjustable telescoping handle in between (page 108, below). When you force the head into the pile at one edge of your carpet, tiny hooks catch the nap and longer teeth reach beneath the pile to the back of the carpet. When you bump the kicking cushion, or pad, with your knee, the knee-kicker shoots forwards, carrying the carpet towards the wall; if you have placed the tool in the correct way, the carpet will remain against the wall, caught by the spikes which protrude from the gripper.

After stretching, the excess carpet round the perimeter is trimmed down until it is only 10 mm oversize; this edge is then tucked into the gap between the gripper and the skirting board. The cut edges are thus hidden and the carpet is securely held in place by the grippers.

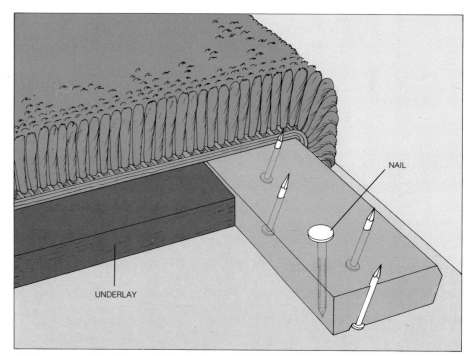

NAIL

UNDERLAY

Holding carpet with grippers. Timber grippers are made of 25 mm wide strips of wood with sharp spikes protruding at a 60-degree angle from the face to grip the carpet. They are fixed to the floor with pre-set nails, with the pins pointing towards the wall. Grippers with masonry nails are available for concrete floors. When carpet is stretched over the gripper, the spikes hold it under tension. The tucked-in edge of the carpet is held in the gully between wall and gripper.

Securing Grippers with Nails

1 **Nailing grippers to the floor.** Starting in a corner, hold a gripper in a gloved hand and nail it in place, slightly less than the thickness of the carpet from the wall. A gap of about 5 mm is usually adequate; as a guide, use a spacer made by gluing cardboard together to the required thickness. Fix the gripper at both ends before you drive in the middle nails—this allows you to flex the gripper to match the alignment of a wall that is bowed. If you find it difficult to avoid hammering down the spikes as you are nailing, use a nail punch. Butt the ends of adjacent strips of gripper tightly together.

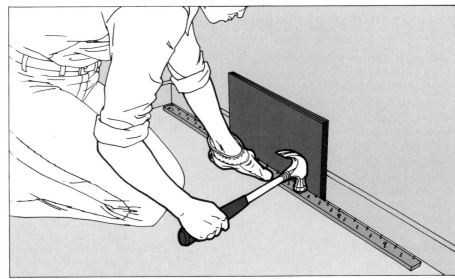

2 **Cutting strip.** With a saw or secateurs, cut short pieces to fill gaps or to fit round bays, built-in furniture or door jambs *(right)*. If you use secateurs, wear goggles in case the cut piece springs up. Grip the strip in the jaws, position the lower handle against the floor and lean on the upper handle to make the cut. At door openings install small pieces to maintain the correct spacing between the strip and each section of moulding. Drive in extra nails so that each piece of strip is held by at least two.

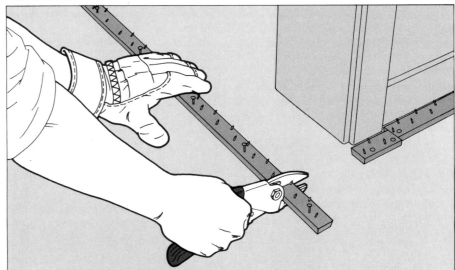

Fastening Grippers with Adhesive

Gluing the gripper. On an uneven, non-nailable surface such as a tiled floor, cut the strip to the width of each tile—if the tiles are very small, cut the strips about 100 mm long and leave a gap of about 3 mm between each strip. Clean and sand the surface, then fasten each strip with contact adhesive. Tap the strip down with a hammer. Caution: provide adequate ventilation when using contact adhesive. Keep the lid on the tin when you are not using it. If the adhesive is inflammable, be sure to extinguish all pilot lights and switch off the electricity supply to any nearby electrical appliances.

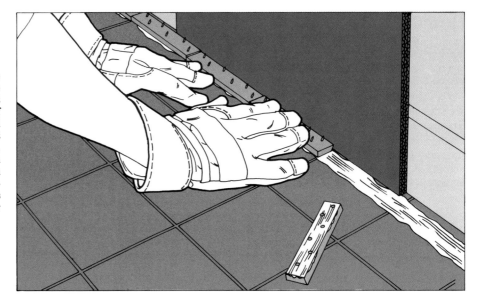

Fitting the Underlay

1 **Securing the underlay.** Using a trimming knife, cut lengths of underlay a few centimetres longer than the width of the room. If necessary, trim the width of the underlay so that the seams between adjacent lengths will not coincide with the planned carpet seams. Butt one end of the first length loosely against the edge of the grippers, then secure it to the floor with staples, pins or double-sided adhesive tape about 200 mm from the wall—if you secure it any closer, the underlay may ruck up when the carpet is stretched over the gripper. To flatten the underlay, shuffle along it until you reach the opposite wall. Secure the free end of the underlay about 200 mm from the wall *(right)*, leaving the last few centimetres overlapping the gripper.

2 **Trimming the overlap.** With a trimming knife, remove the overlap by cutting along the inside edge of the gripper *(right)*.

Butt adjacent lengths of underlay tightly together and secure the seams with single-sided adhesive tape stuck to the top of the underlay.

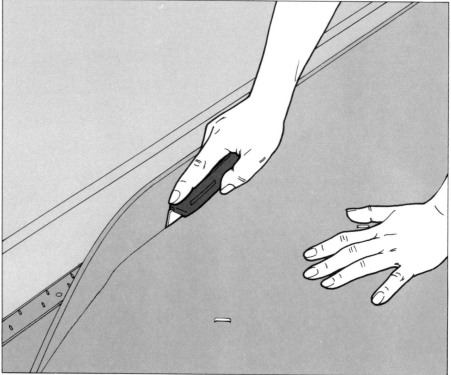

Seaming the Carpet with Webbing

Sticking down the edges. Cut the adjacent sections of carpet and mark the floor along the line of the seam *(page 103, Step 1)*. Fold back the carpet edges and weight them down if necessary.

Lay a strip of webbing on the floor, centring it along the marked line, then use a carpet scrap to smear latex-based adhesive on top of the webbing *(below, left)*. Smear adhesive on to the backing of each folded-back section of carpet, then unfold both carpet edges and gently press them down together on the webbing, smoothing them towards the seam *(below, right)*.

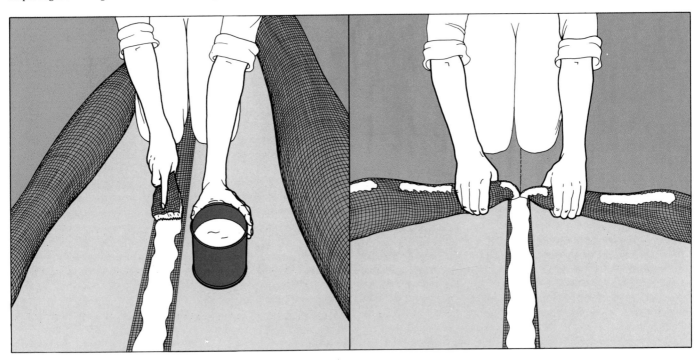

Stretching the Carpet

Using a knee-kicker. Adjust the knob on the head of the knee-kicker until you can just feel the teeth protruding on the underside of a scrap of carpet. Beginning at one corner of the room *(opposite page, above)*, press the head of the kicker on to the carpet about 40 mm away from the wall. Lean on the handle with one hand, steady yourself with the other, and then smartly "kick" the cushioned pad with your knee. The carpet, shoved forwards, should catch on the gripper, and the excess will lap further up the wall. If this does not happen, repeat the process and press the carpet on to the gripper after using the kicker. As you move along a wall, hold the secured carpet in place with your free hand so that it does not come unhooked as you kick.

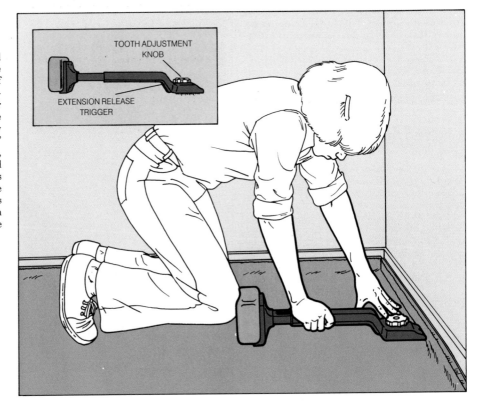

TOOTH ADJUSTMENT KNOB

EXTENSION RELEASE TRIGGER

When and Where to Kick and Stretch

Fitting a taut carpet. These pictures show the sequence in which the knee-kicker should be used to stretch the carpet in a typical room. Begin by hooking the carpet over the gripper in a corner opposite the doorway (1). Then hook it on to the gripper in the corner diagonally opposite (2), and stretch it along the first long wall (3 to 6), using the knee-kicker at a slight angle. Do not stretch it into the loose corner at this stage, but stretch instead along the adjacent wall (7 to 9). Then stretch and secure into the corner (10). Stretch the carpet on to the second long wall (11 to 15) and then along the wall with the doorway (16 to 19). Finally, stretch on to the binder bar in the doorway, using the kicker twice (20 and 21).

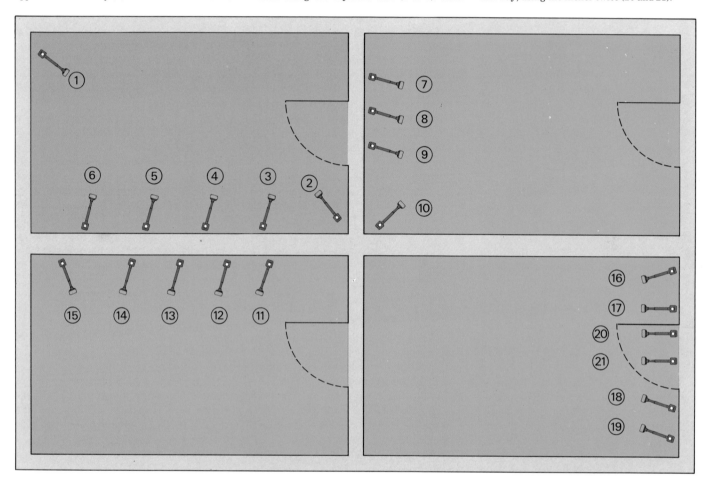

Finishing the Edges

Tucking in the carpet. Trim the edges of the carpet *(page 104, Step 1)*, holding the knife blade at a shallow angle and leaving 10 mm excess carpet all round the perimeter of the room. Use a bolster with a blunt edge to tuck the excess carpet into the gully between the grippers and the skirting board *(right)*. Brush loose strands of yarn out of the gully with the tip of a screwdriver and cut them off if necessary—do not pull them out, as this might cause the carpet to fray. If the carpet edge bulges too much to be tucked in, trim it a little closer.

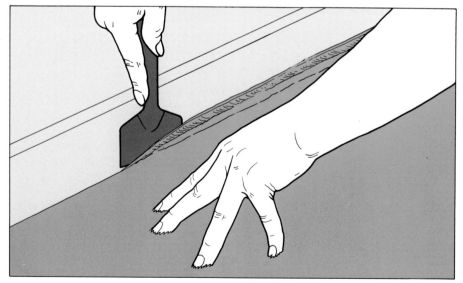

The Right Way to Carpet a Staircase

A staircase is no place to economize on carpeting; it gets too much wear, especially at the nosing of the treads. The nap of a cheap carpet with a low pile density will soon wear away there, exposing the carpet backing in an effect that the carpet trade calls "grinning". Although some types of foam-backed carpet will stand up to the wear, it is safer to use a heavy domestic hessian-backed or woven carpet.

The underlay beneath the carpet must be strong enough to protect the nosings of the stairs and to absorb the impact of heavy footsteps. Use either a waffled rubber type or traditional felt—the cheaper foam underlays are not suitable.

Because footsteps, whether ascending or descending, exert pressure towards the nosing, the pile of the carpet should also run down the stairs, towards the nosing, so that it yields to foot pressure instead of resisting it. (If the pile leans towards the top of the stairs, carpet life may be substantially reduced.)

Carpet is usually laid wall to wall on closed staircases or from a wall to the base of the balusters on staircases with an open side. However, if you wish to lay a carpet that can be removed easily and relaid on another staircase, you can instead install a "runner"—that is, a carpet laid down the centre of the stairs, leaving the sides bare to be painted or polished. If you allow an extra half metre on the length of a runner and tuck this under on the top tread, the carpet can be lifted after a year or so and repositioned on the staircase to even out wear. Secure the turn-under with 25 mm carpet tacks instead of grippers.

When estimating the amount of carpet needed for a staircase, begin by establishing the breadth of carpeting for a straight flight. Measure each step individually, since the width often varies; for an open staircase, add about 50 mm to the maximum width as a tucking-under allowance for the edges *(page 112, Step 3)*. Then measure the entire length of the stairs by running a piece of string from the back of the top tread to the base of the bottom riser, following the profile of each stair; add on an extra 25 mm per step to allow for the depth of the underlay.

If you are using plain broadloom carpet, find out how many pieces you will be able to cut from a standard roll by dividing its width by the breadth of stair carpet required. (If the carpet is patterned, allow for wastage: the pattern should be centred on the stairs, and must be matched up with the hall or landing carpet.) To calculate the number of running metres of broadloom carpet needed, divide the length of the staircase by the number of widths you can cut from a standard roll. This is only a rough estimation; the final figure may be somewhat higher, because two separate lengths of carpet must always meet at a tread-riser angle. Each piece, therefore, must run from an upper end at the back of a tread to a lower end at the bottom of a riser. Check your sections of carpet carefully for this fit and add an additional length if necessary. When you begin cutting the carpet, use the method appropriate to its type as described on page 99.

A landing carpet is measured, cut and installed in the same way as floor carpet, but to avoid a dangerously placed seam it must also cover the first riser down from the landing. Fasten the riser portion at the bottom of the riser before stretching the carpet over the landing. Stairs with a half-landing should be treated as two separate flights; if possible, use a single length of carpet to cover both the lower flight and the half-landing.

When a staircase winds round a corner, the best way to determine the amount of carpet you will need for its wedge-shaped steps, called winders, is to cut paper templates. Each winder step will be carpeted separately and each template should cover one tread and the riser underneath it. Add an additional 25 mm to the depth of a template to allow for the bulge of underlay over the nosing of the treads, and the same to its width to allow for turning under on an open side.

When cutting the carpet for a winder step, set the template so its bottom edge aligns with the weft, or cross threads, of the carpet. The warp, or lengthways threads, will run vertically up the riser and break squarely over the nosing, making the carpet less vulnerable to wear. When installing the piece, attach it to the gripper on the riser; stretch it over the tread. A closed side of a winder tread is carpeted on grippers like a landing. If the wall has a pronounced curve, cut the gripper into small pieces that follow the arc. On an open side, roll the carpet edge under and tack it into place at the back of the tread.

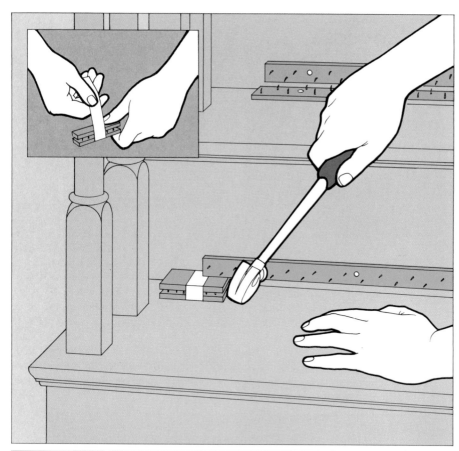

1 Installing the gripper. Cut a strip of gripper *(page 106)* 50 mm shorter than the width of a step and nail the strip to the riser with its pins pointing down. To position the strip at the correct distance above the tread, rest it on spacers made by pulling the nails from short pieces of gripper and tapping the strips together, pins to pins *(inset)*. Nail gripper cut to the same length to the tread, 15 mm from the riser, with the pins of this strip pointing towards the riser. Repeat the process for each riser and tread.

2 Installing the underlay. Cut a piece of underlay 50 mm shorter than the width of a step, butt it flush to the gripper and staple or pin it on to the tread; then pull it over the nose of the step and staple it about 75 mm down the riser. If one side of the staircase is open, cut the riser portion of the underlay away from the nosing at an angle on the open side so that it will not be seen when carpet is installed.

3 **Preparing the edges.** If the staircase is open, cut the carpet 50 mm wider than the breadth of the stairs and lay it face down. Snap chalk lines 25 mm from each side to mark the crease for the turnover, and score the back of the carpet along the chalked lines with an awl or the back of a trimming knife. As you score the lines, fold the carpet edges over with your fingers *(right)*.

For a closed staircase, cut the carpet to the maximum width of the stairs and trim off any excess on narrower stairs as you lay the carpet. To prevent fraying, apply a thin bead of latex-based adhesive to the cut edges of the carpet backing.

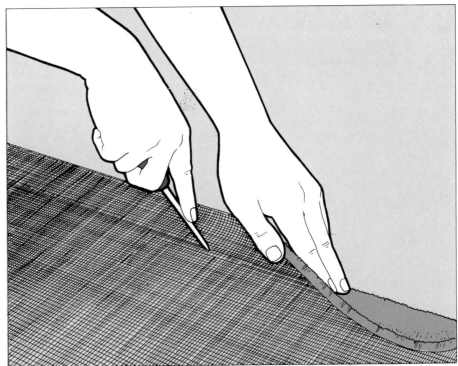

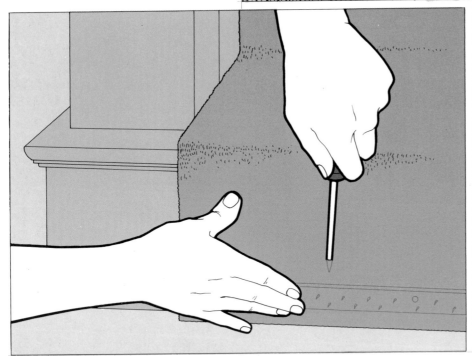

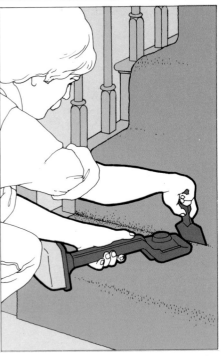

4 **Securing the bottom edge.** Unroll the carpet down the stairs from the top tread, using a blunt bolster to force it into the tread-riser angle at the centre of each step. Pull the edge down over the gripper on the bottom riser, using an awl if necessary, until about 10 mm laps on to the floor. Press the carpet on to the pins with your fingers and iron along it with the flat side of a bolster. Use the bolster to tuck the excess into the gully between the gripper and floor. Secure the turned-under edges with a 25 mm carpet through the carpet and into the bottom of the riser on each side.

5 **Covering the tread.** Stretch the carpet over the bottom tread with a knee-kicker and, at the same time, push it into the space behind the gripper with a bolster; the pins of the gripper at the back of the tread should grip and hold the carpet backing. Begin this step of the job at the centre of the tread and stretch the carpet directly back towards the stair riser; then work the carpet outwards towards the edges of the stair tread. For this part of the job, the knee-kicker should be angled away from the centre.

6 **Adjusting a turned-under edge.** If the width of a tread varies from step to step or from front to back on a single step, push an awl through the top layer of the carpet's turned-under edge, pierce the lower layer with the tip and, using the awl like a lever, shift the turned-under edge to make the carpet fit the width at every point.

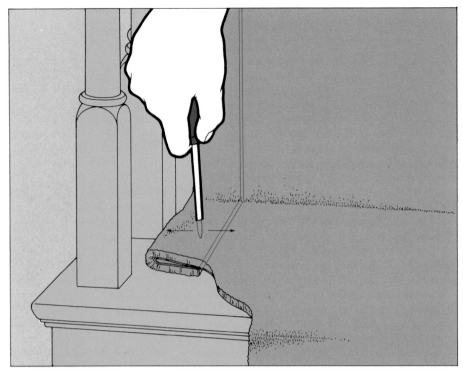

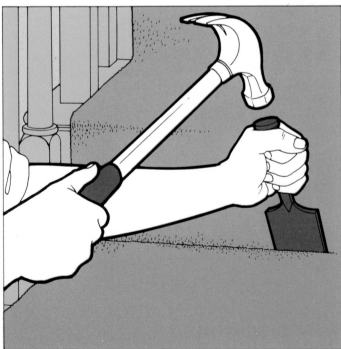

7 **Forcing the carpet into the stair angle.** Using a bolster and a hammer, drive the carpet into the space between the grippers on the tread and riser along the full width of the stair. By doing this, you will tighten the carpet over the tread and also fix the carpet to the gripper on the riser.

8 **Tacking at the edges.** Secure turned-under edges at the tread-riser angle with 25 mm carpet tacks driven through the carpet and into the angle of the stair at each side.

You are now ready to stretch the carpet on the treads above. When you reach the end of a length of carpet, drive a tack through each turned-under edge into the back of the tread, trim off any excess carpet with a trimming knife and fit the next piece to the next riser *(Step 4)*.

Unseen Repairs for Stains and Tears

The most carefully tended carpets can suffer accidental damage. The flick of a cigarette can cause small but noticeable burns. The sharp edge of a broken toy cuts through the pile of a carpet or rips its backing. And stains from some liquids stubbornly resist shampoos and spot removers. But with a few scraps of matching carpet and some inexpensive tools and materials, it is possible to make durable, almost invisible repairs.

Set scraps aside whenever you lay a carpet or ask for some from the seller if you are buying a carpeted house. If no scraps have been saved, take them from unseen areas such as within built-in cupboards.

Small areas of damage can be repaired by retufting (below and opposite). If you have no spare scraps of carpet, pick out individual replacement tufts from round the perimeter of the carpet or from tucked-down edges. The new tufts are sewn into the carpet with a half-round needle and carpet thread; if necessary, you can heat a straight needle in a flame and then bend it into a suitable curved shape.

Larger areas of damage have to be patched. To avoid damaging the pile, woven carpets must be folded back and the patch sewn in from the back (pages 116–117). Patch tufted carpets from the top, using webbing and heavy-duty, latex-based adhesive (pages 118–119).

Surface rips, which have pulled the top layer of carpet away from its backing, are repaired from the top with adhesive (page 119, below); any bare patches round the edges of the rip should then be retufted. Tears which have cut through the carpet backing must be repaired from the back (page 120). You should never stick tape on the top of the carpet as a temporary measure—it is impossible to remove the tape without damaging the pile.

Although most carpet repairs are not difficult to make, they demand patience. When you are replacing tufts, for example, do not attempt to hurry the work; the best results will come from building up the pile over the damaged area carefully, one tuft at a time. Apply latex adhesive sparingly, so that no excess oozes on to the surface of the carpet. Before you cut a patch, make sure that it will match the pattern and the direction of the pile in the damaged area.

You should always use your smallest piece of scrap carpet first, so that if you make an error, there will be larger scraps available to correct it. And when you embark upon a job that is new to you, take the time to practise on unneeded scraps of carpet before tackling the real thing.

Preparing for retufting. Using scissors with short, curved blades—a pair of ordinary cuticle scissors will do—cut the damaged pile down to the carpet backing, then pick out the stubs of the tufts or loops with tweezers. To remove stubborn pile, dab the carpet backing at the foot of the tufts or loops with a cotton-wool bud dipped in petrol, which softens the adhesive that anchors the pile to the backing. For replacement pile, pick tufts or unravel lengths of looped yarn from the edge of a carpet scrap.

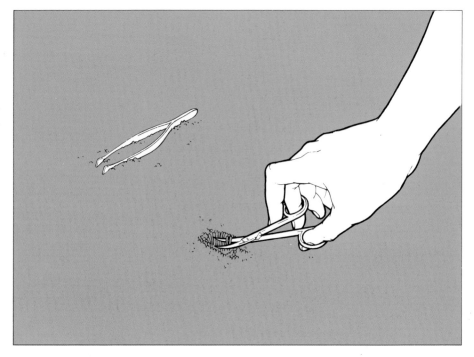

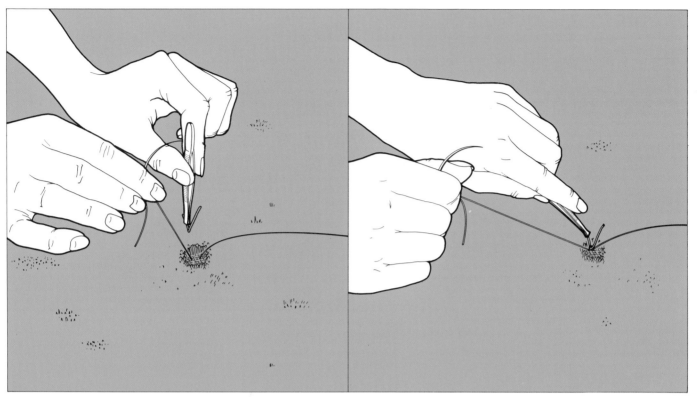

Replacing cut-pile tufts. Push back the pile round the shaven area to expose the backing. Thread a half-round needle with carpet thread. Holding the short end of a replacement tuft with tweezers, pull the needle through one of the strands in the exposed backing *(above, left)*, and loop it back over the V of the tuft. Repeat the first stitch through the backing and pull the thread gently to anchor the tuft *(above, right)*. Without cutting the thread, sew a second tuft on to an adjacent strand in the backing, and continue until the exposed area is completely covered. Knot the carpet thread round the last strand to anchor it. On secondary-backed carpets, separate the new pile and dab the backing with a cotton-wool bud dipped in petrol to ensure that the backing adhesive adheres to the new tufts. Trim any uneven tufts with scissors.

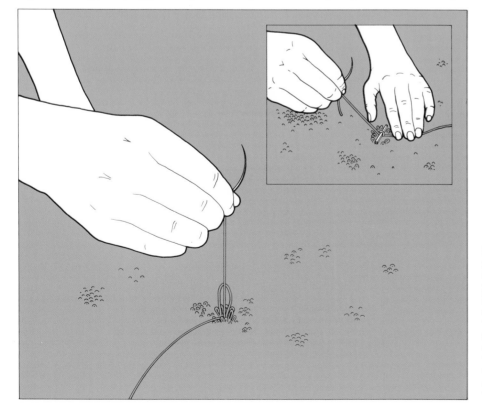

Replacing loop-pile tufts. Press back the pile round the shaven area. Using a half-round needle, thread a length of unravelled carpet yarn through one of the strands in the exposed backing, then repeat the stitch to make a loop in the yarn. Tighten the loop to match those on the surrounding carpet, using a matchstick or similar object inserted through the loop to standardize its size *(inset)*. Repeat the looped stitch through the next strand in the backing without cutting the yarn, and continue until the whole area has been rewoven. Secure the yarn ends by threading them through the backing.

Patching a Woven Carpet

1 Loosening the carpet. Using a knee-kicker *(page 108)*, reduce the tension of the carpet at the corner of the room closest to the area that requires patching. Lift the carpet from the hooks of the gripper with an awl. When the corner is free, use your hands to pull the carpet from the gripper along the two walls.

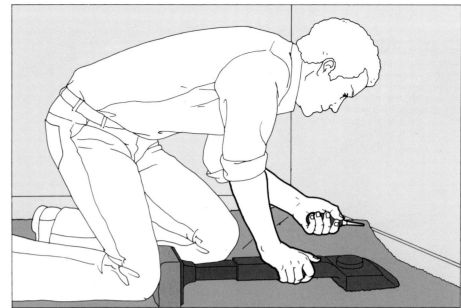

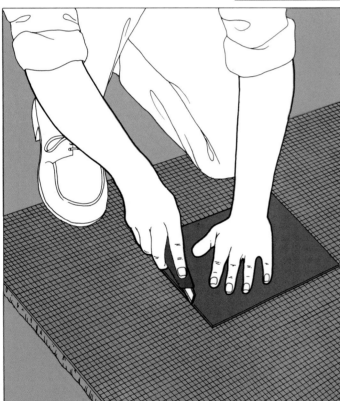

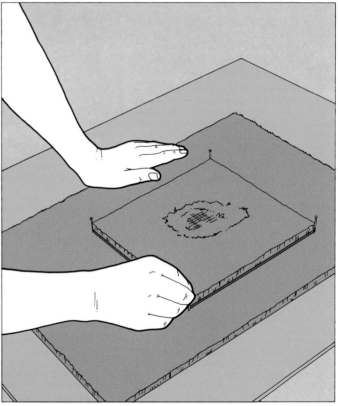

2 Cutting out the damaged area. Mark the corners of the damaged area on the face of the carpet by sticking pins through both pile and backing. Cut a hardboard or stiff cardboard template to fit the marked area, then fold back the loosened carpet to expose the underside. Position the template on the underside of the carpet so that its edges run parallel to the lines of the carpet weave. Taking care to cut through the backing only, cut along the edges of the template with a trimming knife.

3 Cutting the replacement patch. Place the cut-out patch of carpet on top of an unused carpet scrap. Match up the pile directions and, for a patterned carpet, the patterns on both pieces of carpet, then stick pins through the scrap carpet at the corners of the cut-out patch *(right)*. Remove the cut-out patch and turn over the scrap piece, then cut out the replacement patch using the template as described in Step 2.

4 **Inserting the patch.** To prevent fraying, apply a thin bead of adhesive to the carpet backing round the edge of the replacement patch and round the perimeter of the hole cut in the floor carpet; take care not to get adhesive on the pile. Match up the pile directions—and, if applicable, the patterns—of the replacement patch and the floor carpet. Starting at one corner and working towards the corner diagonally opposite, gently press the replacement patch into position. Use the blunt end of a needle to push down any pile sticking up round the edge of the patch.

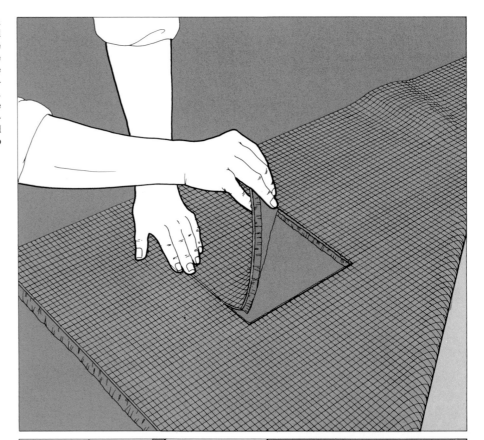

5 **Sewing in the patch.** Ensure that the edges of the patch and the surrounding carpet are exactly aligned. Press two adjoining edges together in a slight peak and sew them together with a flat needle and carpet thread, using alternate long (30 mm) and short (20 mm) stitches. Check the face of the carpet frequently to ensure that no pile is caught up by the thread. Continue sewing round the remaining edges of the patch, then fold back the carpet and stretch it on to the grippers with a knee-kicker. Weight the patched area with a pile of books for a few hours so that the pile spreads and merges with the surrounding carpet.

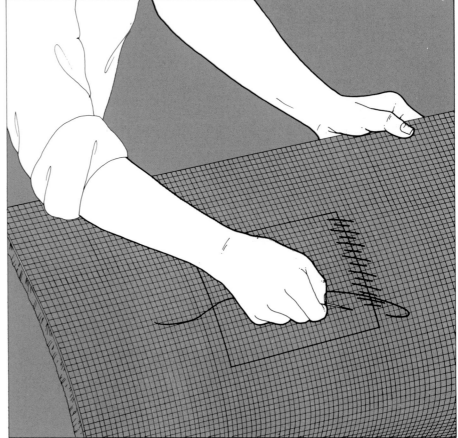

Patching a Tufted Carpet

1 Stay tacking a carpet. If the carpet is secured with grippers, lay strips of scrap carpet pile-side down about 200 mm from the edges of the damaged area and secure them with 25 mm carpet tacks at intervals of about 75 mm. This procedure, known as "stay tacking", reduces the tension over the area to be cut out. If the carpet is secured with adhesive tape or is loose laid, stay tacking is not necessary.

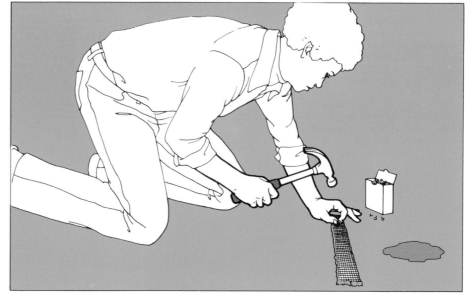

2 Cutting out the damaged area. Cut a hardboard template to the size of the damaged area and position it on the carpet. Separate the pile round the edges of the template with the back of a trimming knife blade, then force the pile apart with your fingers. Cut through the carpet backing round the template, taking care not to cut through any underlay, then prise up the cut area at one corner and gently lift the patch out.

Cut a replacement patch from scrap carpet, using the cut-out patch to match pile direction and pattern and the hardboard template to guide the cutting lines.

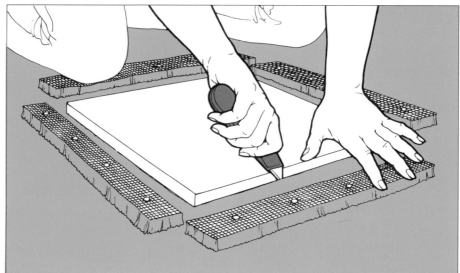

3 Placing the seam tape. The patch will be held by webbing tape slipped part of the way under the carpet. Cut four strips of webbing tape about 25 mm longer than the sides of the hole and coat the strips with thin layers of latex seam adhesive (use just enough to fill in the weave of the tape). Slip the strips beneath the edges of the hole so that a cut edge of the carpet lies over the centre line of each strip. Squeeze a thin bead of adhesive along the edges of the carpet backing, but avoid getting any adhesive on the pile.

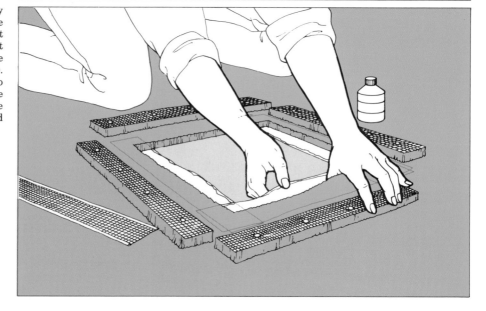

4 **Securing the patch.** Align the pile direction and pattern of the replacement patch with the surrounding carpet. Starting at one corner and working towards the one diagonally opposite, press the patch gently into the hole, taking care not to smear the pile with adhesive. Push the edges of patch and carpet together with your fingers and press on the seams round the patch with the heels of your hands. Use an awl to free any tufts or loops of pile crushed into the seam, and brush your fingers back and forth across the seams to blend the pile of carpet and patch. Weight the patch with a pile of books for a few hours.

On a carpet secured with grippers, ease out stay tacks round the patch after about five hours and restore the carpet tension with a knee-kicker.

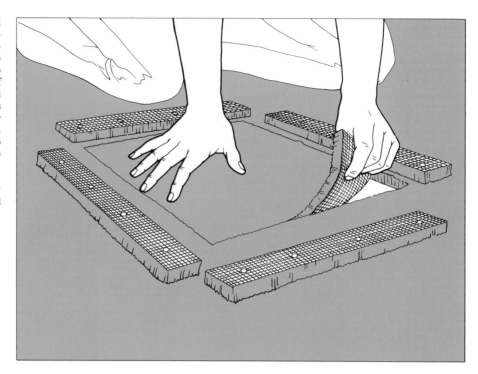

Mending a Surface Rip

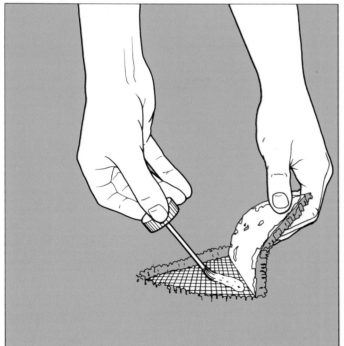

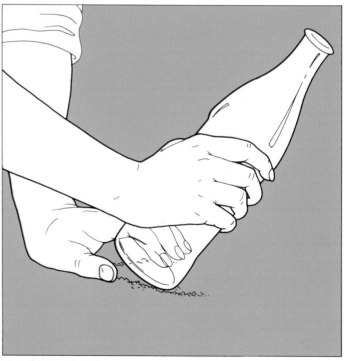

1 **Applying adhesive.** If the backing is undamaged, lift the torn section of carpet face away from it, clean out any loose pile and apply latex seam adhesive to the backing. Smear the adhesive into a light film over all of the exposed backing.

2 **Closing the rip.** Push the edges of the rip together and hold them in place with one hand while you rub the carpet surface with a smooth object, such as the bottom of a soft-drink bottle. Rub firmly from the rip towards the sound carpet to work the adhesive well into the fibres of the backing without forcing it out of the rip. If any adhesive does ooze up to the surface, clean it off immediately with water and carpet shampoo. After four or five hours, when the adhesive has dried, replace any missing pile *(pages 114–115)*.

Repairing Tears

Stitching a woven carpet. Use a knee-kicker and awl to lift the carpet off the grippers at one corner *(page 116, Step 1)*, then fold the carpet back to expose the tear on the underside. Holding the torn edges together in a slight peak, use a flat needle and carpet thread to make alternate 30 and 20 mm stitches as described on page 117, Step 5. Cut a piece of webbing tape long enough to cover the tear and coat it with a thin layer of latex adhesive; leave the tape for a few minutes until the adhesive becomes tacky, then press it firmly into position over the stitched edges of the carpet backing. Fold the carpet back into place and re-attach it to the grippers with a knee-kicker.

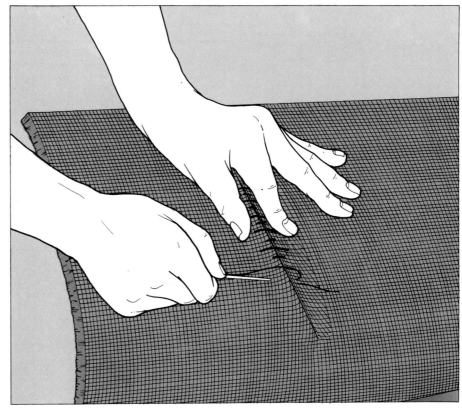

Using adhesive tape. Foam-backed and other tufted carpets can be repaired with either single-sided adhesive tape *(right)* or webbing tape and adhesive. Lift the carpet from the grippers *(page 116, Step 1)* or pull the double-sided adhesive tape from the floor, and fold the carpet back. Match up the edges of the tear, then centre and press into position a length of single-sided adhesive tape about 50 mm wide to cover both edges. Leave for a couple of hours, then straighten the carpet and secure it using grippers or, in the case of foam-backed carpet, double-sided adhesive tape.

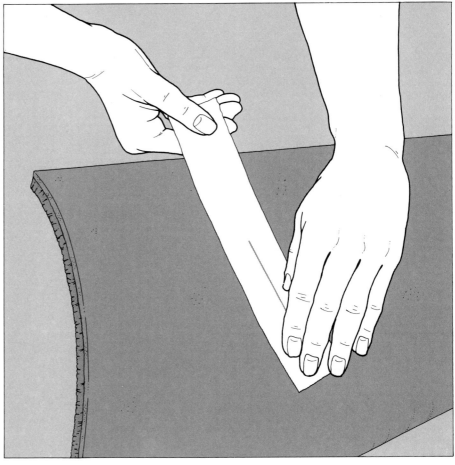

Keeping Carpets Spotless

Routine carpet care requires common-sense procedures. Vacuum at least once a week to remove surface dirt and grit; on looped-pile berber carpets, use a cylinder machine if possible, as most upright vacuums contain a beater bar that flattens and mats this type of pile. Rearrange furniture occasionally and use mats or rugs to reduce wear on specific areas. To avoid fading, protect carpets from strong sunlight by drawing blinds or curtains. Once a year, or more often if required, clean the carpet using one of the methods which are described on pages 122–123.

Deal with any accidental spillages at once—the longer they are left, the more likely it is that the stain will become permanent. Blot up spilt liquids with a clean white absorbent cloth and scrape up solids with a blunt knife, then consult the chart on the right for the correct cleaning agent and technique to use.

Finding the right treatment. In the alphabetized column on the left of this chart, find the material that has stained your carpet and treat it by the method given in the right-hand column. You may have to apply several cleaning solutions in succession. In each case, blot and leave the first solution to dry for one to two hours before applying the second. The cleaning agents specified are as follows:
☐ Dry cleaner. Use a proprietary dry cleaning solvent or white spirit. Caution: most solvents are inflammable and give off toxic fumes. Extinguish any naked lights and ensure that the room is well ventilated.
☐ Shampoo. Proprietary carpet shampoo can be bought in liquid or dry foam crystalline form, and should be used strictly according to the manufacturer's instructions. To make a homemade shampoo, add a teaspoon of mild detergent to 250 ml of lukewarm water; do not use strong detergents or any containing bleach or brightening agents. To prevent dyes in the carpet from bleeding, add one teaspoon of white vinegar to the shampoo solution.
☐ Ammonia. Add one tablespoon of clear household ammonia to one cup of warm water.

To apply any stain remover, wet a clean white pad in the solution and blot it into the stain, dabbing from the edge towards the centre. Always follow a shampoo solution by sponging with water. Finally, cover the spot with white paper towels weighted with a book, leave for five to six hours, then vacuum.

Treatments for Every Stain

Cause of stain	Treatment
Alcoholic beverages	Apply shampoo. If traces remain, apply dry cleaner.
Blood	Sponge with cold water, then apply shampoo. Blot and leave to dry. Apply ammonia solution.
Butter, margarine	Apply dry cleaner.
Candle wax	Cover with brown paper and iron with medium hot iron until wax melts. Then apply dry cleaner.
Chewing gum	Chill with ice cube until brittle, then scrape up with blunt knife. Apply dry cleaner. If traces remain, apply shampoo.
Chocolate, sweets	Apply shampoo. If traces remain, apply dry cleaner.
Coffee, tea	Apply shampoo, then ammonia solution. If traces remain, apply dry cleaner.
Crayons	Apply dry cleaner and then shampoo.
Egg	Apply shampoo and follow with ammonia solution.
Excrement	Sponge with cool water. Apply shampoo followed by ammonia solution.
Fruit, fruit juices	Apply shampoo followed by ammonia solution. If traces remain, apply dry cleaner.
Furniture polish	Apply dry cleaner and then shampoo.
Gravy	Apply shampoo followed by ammonia solution. If traces remain, apply dry cleaner.
Grease	Apply dry cleaner.
Ink, washable	Apply mild detergent.
Lipstick	Apply dry cleaner, then shampoo.
Milk, ice cream	Apply shampoo. If grease stain then appears, apply dry cleaner.
Motor oil	Apply dry cleaner followed by lukewarm water, then shampoo and then ammonia solution.
Mud	Let dry, brush gently, vacuum, then apply shampoo.
Mustard	Apply shampoo. If traces remain, apply dry cleaner.
Paint, wet oil-based	Apply dry cleaner.
Paint, wet water-based	Blot dry. Apply shampoo.
Perfume	Apply shampoo and then dry cleaner.
Salad dressing	Apply dry cleaner. If traces remain, apply shampoo.
Shoe polish	Apply dry cleaner, then shampoo followed by ammonia solution.
Soft drinks	Apply shampoo and then ammonia solution. If traces remain, apply dry cleaner.
Syrup	Apply dry cleaner.
Urine	Apply shampoo, then ammonia solution and, if necessary, more shampoo.
Vegetable oil	Apply dry cleaner. If traces remain, apply shampoo.
Vomit	Sponge with cool water. Apply shampoo and then ammonia solution.

Two Ways to Launder a Carpet by Machine

About once a year—or more often if they need it—you should clean your carpets thoroughly. This can be done manually with a carpet shampoo or with one of the two types of electric cleaning machines: a foam-action shampooer like the one shown on the right, or the more efficient water-extraction cleaner illustrated on the opposite page. Both machines can be hired; allow about a day to clean all the carpets in an average three-bedroomed house.

Shampooers vary in design but usually consist of a dispensing tank on the handle, in which tap water and detergent are mixed in specified proportions, and rotating motorized brushes which work the mixture into the carpet. The shampoo foam loosens particles of dirt and dries to a crystalline form round them; you then vacuum up both foam and dirt. Use only the recommended detergent or a proprietary carpet shampoo; other household detergents require rinsing and may leave a sticky film that quickly attracts dirt.

Shampooing is easier and less expensive than water extraction, but repeated shampooing leaves a build-up of detergent residue. Some professionals do not recommend shampooers at all; if you do use one, switch to a water-extraction machine instead at least every third cleaning, to remove the detergent residue.

Water-extraction machines operate by spraying a non-foaming detergent solution on to the carpet under pressure and immediately sucking up at least 90 per cent of the solution—and the dirt—from the carpet. To accomplish this, an extraction machine has two electric pumps as well as a dispensing and waste tank. The machine is prepared by filling the solution tank to a specified level with hand-hot water (hotter water could damage the carpet). The detergent is added as recommended by the manufacturer—usually 350 millilitres for a full tank. The waste tank should be rinsed clean if necessary and then part-filled with a defoamer in order to neutralize excess foaming.

If possible, choose a warm, breezy day to do your cleaning and keep the room well ventilated to encourage fast drying. Remove as much furniture as you can and, to avoid staining the carpet with rust marks, protect the metal feet of remaining furniture with kitchen foil or greaseproof paper.

Vacuum the carpet thoroughly and spot-clean as described on page 121. Test a small patch of the carpet for colour-fastness with a rag dipped into the cleaning solution before you begin—carpets containing natural dyes are particularly prone to bleeding when shampooed.

When either shampooing or cleaning by water extraction, be careful not to overwet the carpet and go easy on the solution-dispensing trigger. Excess water can cause the carpet's jute backing to shrink and pull the carpet from its fastenings. It can also dissolve the colours in the backing and underlay, which then rise to the carpet surface and leave a stain.

Carpets cleaned by water extraction will usually be dry enough to walk on within a couple of hours. Shampooed carpets should be left overnight before the dried foam and dirt is vacuumed up. If you have to move furniture back into the room before the carpet is completely dry, wrap any metal feet or castors in foil or plastic bags.

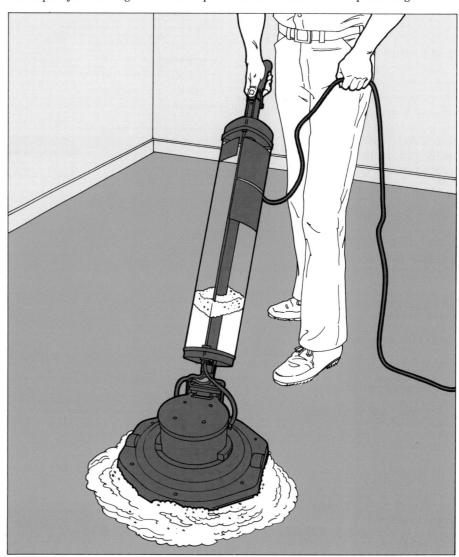

Shampooing. With the brushes rotating, push the shampooer over an area about 1 metre square while pressing the trigger to release detergent solution. Then go over the area again without releasing detergent, scrubbing the foam into the carpet. Repeat this process over several areas, then brush the carpet lightly in the direction of the pile with a long-handled broom. When the entire room has been shampooed, leave the carpet to dry overnight and then vacuum thoroughly.

Water-extraction cleaning. Switch on the machine's pump and, starting in one corner and working towards the door, hold the vacuum head flat on the carpet and pull it towards you while squeezing the spray-release trigger. Move slowly and steadily; no downward pressure is necessary. At the end of each stroke, release the trigger but continue moving the vacuum head a little further to pick up any drops. Run the head over the same area two more times without spraying, so that the vacuum removes any remaining solution. Repeat this process over the entire carpet, slightly overlapping strokes to avoid a streaky appearance. If a strip does not look clean, spray and vacuum again, but do not spray an area more than twice without letting it dry.

When the solution tank runs empty or the waste tank is full, switch off the machine, drain and rinse the waste tank, then fill both tanks again as directed and resume the operation.

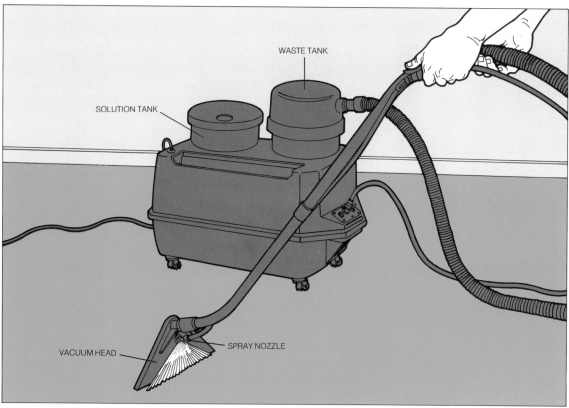

WASTE TANK

SOLUTION TANK

VACUUM HEAD

SPRAY NOZZLE

Cleaning stair carpet. If you cannot hire a water-extraction machine with stair-climbing wheels or an extra-long hose, clean stairs by hand. Make foam by squeezing a sponge repeatedly in carpet shampoo solution, scoop up some of it with a clean scrubbing brush and work the foam into the carpet. Wring out the sponge in the shampoo solution and wipe up the excess foam. Brush or rake the pile erect, leave the carpet to dry overnight, then go over it again with a stiff brush to loosen dried foam and dirt. Finally, vacuum.

Picture Credits

The sources for the illustrations in this book are shown below. Credits for the illustrations from left to right are separated by semicolons, from top to bottom by dashes.

Cover: John Elliott. 6: John Elliott. 8–14: Drawings by Oxford Illustrators Ltd. 15: Drawing by Fred Bigio from B-C Graphics—drawings by Oxford Illustrators Ltd.—drawing by Fred Bigio from B-C Graphics. 16–21: Drawings by Oxford Illustrators Ltd. 22: Drawing by Walter Hilmers Jr. 23: Drawing by Walter Hilmers Jr.—drawing by Walter Hilmers Jr.; drawing by Oxford Illustrators Ltd.—drawing by Walter Hilmers Jr. 24: Drawing by Oxford Illustrators Ltd.—drawing by Walter Hilmers Jr. 25: Drawings by Walter Hilmers Jr. 26–33: Drawings by Peter McGinn. 34: John Elliott. 36–38: Drawings by Oxford Illustrators Ltd. 39: Drawing by Oxford Illustrators Ltd.—drawing by Ray Skibinski. 40: Drawings by Oxford Illustrators Ltd. 41: Drawing by Oxford Illustrators Ltd.—drawings by Ray Skibinski. 42: Drawings by Ray Skibinski.

43: Drawing by Ray Skibinski—Drawing by Oxford Illustrators Ltd. 44, 45: Drawings by Ray Skibinski. 47–49: Drawings by Fred Bigio from B-C Graphics. 50, 51: Drawings by Peter McGinn. 52, 53: Drawings by Whitman Studio, Inc. 54: Drawing by Oxford Illustrators Ltd.; drawing by Whitman Studio, Inc.—drawing by Whitman Studio, Inc. 55: Drawings by Whitman Studio, Inc. 56–61: Drawings by Oxford Illustrators Ltd. 62: Fred Maroon. 64: Drawing by Oxford Illustrators Ltd. 65: Drawing by Oxford Illustrators Ltd.—drawings by Vantage Art, Inc. 66, 67: Drawings by Vantage Art, Inc. 68: Drawings by Vantage Art, Inc. 69: Drawing by Vantage Art, Inc.—drawings by Vantage Art, Inc.; drawing by Oxford Illustrators Ltd. 70, 71: Drawings by Vantage Art, Inc. 72: Drawing by Vantage Art, Inc.—drawings by Oxford Illustrators Ltd. 73: Drawings by Vantage Art, Inc. 74—79: Drawings by Oxford Illustrators Ltd. 80, 81: Drawings by Walter Hilmers Jr. 82, 83: Drawings by Oxford Illustrators Ltd. 84: Drawing by Walter Hilmers Jr.—drawing

by Walter Hilmers Jr.; drawing by Oxford Illustrators Ltd. 85–93: Drawings by Oxford Illustrators Ltd. 94: Fred Maroon. 96, 97: Drawings by Great, Inc. 98: Drawing by Oxford Illustrators Ltd. 99: Drawing by Oxford Illustrators Ltd.—drawing by Great, Inc. 100: Drawing by Great Inc.—drawings by Oxford Illustrators Ltd. 101: Drawings by Oxford Illustrators Ltd. 102: Drawing by Great, Inc.—drawings by Oxford Illustrators Ltd. 103, 104: Drawings by Oxford Illustrators Ltd. 105—107: Drawings by Great, Inc. 108: Drawings by Oxford Illustrators Ltd.—drawing by Great, Inc. 109: Drawings by Oxford Illustrators Ltd.—drawing by Great, Inc. 111–113: Drawings by Ray Skibinski. 114: Drawing by Peter McGinn. 115: Drawings by Oxford Illustrators Ltd. 116: Drawing by Peter McGinn—drawings by Oxford Illustrators Ltd. 117: Drawings by Oxford Illustrators Ltd. 118, 119: Drawings by Peter McGinn. 120: Drawing by Ray Skibinski—drawing by Oxford Illustrators Ltd. 122, 123: Drawings by Dick Gage.

Acknowledgements

The editors would like to extend special thanks to Neil Fairbairn, Tim Fraser, Liz Hodgson, Caroline Manyon, Andy Monks and Mike Snell, London. They also wish to thank the following: H. Burbidge, Oswestry, Salop.; Calaora Carpet Co., London; Greg Callaghan, Sydney; Chipboard Promotion Association, Marlow, Bucks.; Roland Chomel, Grenoble; Jim Dossetter, London; J.M. Goodacre, Boulton and Paul Joinery Ltd., Melton Mowbray, Leics.; Alan Goodwin, Kalletal-Talle; Simon Jolley, Building Adhesives Ltd., Stoke on Trent, Staffs.; Martin Long, London; Magnet and Southern Joinery, London; Patent Steam Cleaning Co. Ltd., London; Vicki Robinson, London; Timber Research and Development Association, High Wycombe, Bucks.

Index/Glossary

Metric Conversion Chart

Approximate equivalents—length

Millimetres to inches		Inches to millimetres	
1	$\frac{1}{32}$	$\frac{1}{32}$	1
2	$\frac{1}{16}$	$\frac{1}{16}$	2
3	$\frac{1}{8}$	$\frac{1}{8}$	3
4	$\frac{5}{32}$	$\frac{3}{16}$	5
5	$\frac{3}{16}$	$\frac{1}{4}$	6
6	$\frac{1}{4}$	$\frac{5}{16}$	8
7	$\frac{9}{32}$	$\frac{3}{8}$	10
8	$\frac{5}{16}$	$\frac{7}{16}$	11
9	$\frac{11}{32}$	$\frac{1}{2}$	13
10 (1cm)	$\frac{3}{8}$	$\frac{9}{16}$	14
11	$\frac{7}{16}$	$\frac{5}{8}$	16
12	$\frac{15}{32}$	$\frac{11}{16}$	17
13	$\frac{1}{2}$	$\frac{3}{4}$	19
14	$\frac{9}{16}$	$\frac{13}{16}$	21
15	$\frac{19}{32}$	$\frac{7}{8}$	22
16	$\frac{5}{8}$	$\frac{15}{16}$	24
17	$\frac{11}{16}$	1	25
18	$\frac{23}{32}$	2	51
19	$\frac{3}{4}$	3	76
20	$\frac{25}{32}$	4	102
25	1	5	127
30	$1\frac{3}{16}$	6	152
40	$1\frac{9}{16}$	7	178
50	$1\frac{31}{32}$	8	203
60	$2\frac{3}{8}$	9	229
70	$2\frac{3}{4}$	10	254
80	$3\frac{5}{32}$	11	279
90	$3\frac{9}{16}$	12 (1ft)	305
100	$3\frac{15}{16}$	13	330
200	$7\frac{7}{8}$	14	356
300	$11\frac{13}{16}$	15	381
400	$15\frac{3}{4}$	16	406
500	$19\frac{11}{16}$	17	432
600	$23\frac{5}{8}$	18	457
700	$27\frac{9}{16}$	19	483
800	$31\frac{1}{2}$	20	508
900	$35\frac{7}{16}$	24 (2ft)	610
1000 (1m)	$39\frac{3}{8}$		

Metres to feet/inches		Yards to metres	
		1	0.914
2	6' 7"	2	1.83
3	9' 10"	3	2.74
4	13' 1"	4	3.66
5	16' 5"	5	4.57
6	19' 8"	6	5.49
7	23' 0"	7	6.40
8	26' 3"	8	7.32
9	29' 6"	9	8.23
10	32' 10"	10	9.14
20	65' 7"	20	18.29
50	164' 0"	50	45.72
100	328' 1"	100	91.44

Conversion factors

Length

1 millimetre (mm)	= 0.0394 in
1 centimetre (cm)/10 mm	= 0.3937 in
1 metre/100 cm	= 39.37 in/3.281 ft/1.094 yd
1 kilometre (km)/1000 metres	= 1093.6 yd/0.6214 mile
1 inch (in)	= 25.4 mm/2.54 cm
1 foot (ft)/12 in	= 304.8 mm/30.48 cm/0.3048 metre
1 yard (yd)/3 ft	= 914.4 mm/91.44 cm/0.9144 metre
1 mile/1760 yd	= 1609.344 metres/1.609 km

Area

1 square centimetre (sq cm)/ 100 square millimetres (sq mm)	= 0.155 sq in
1 square metre (sq metre)/10,000 sq cm	= 10.764 sq ft/1.196 sq yd
1 are/100 sq metres	= 119.60 sq yd/0.0247 acre
1 hectare (ha)/100 ares	= 2.471 acres/0.00386 sq mile
1 square inch (sq in)	= 645.16 sq mm/6.4516 sq cm
1 square foot (sq ft)/144 sq in	= 929.03 sq cm
1 square yard (sq yd)/9 sq ft	= 8361.3 sq cm/0.8361 sq metre
1 acre/4840 sq yd	= 4046.9 sq metres/0.4047 ha
1 square mile/640 acres	= 259 ha/2.59 sq km

Volume

1 cubic centimetre (cu cm)/ 1000 cubic millimetres (cu mm)	= 0.0610 cu in
1 cubic decimetre (cu dm)/1000 cu cm	= 61.024 cu in/0.0353 cu ft
1 cubic metre/1000 cu dm	= 35.3147 cu ft/1.308 cu yd
1 cu cm	= 1 millilitre (ml)
1 cu dm	= 1 litre see **Capacity**
1 cubic inch (cu in)	= 16.3871 cu cm
1 cubic foot (cu ft)/1728 cu in	= 28,316.8 cu cm/0·0283 cu metre
1 cubic yard (cu yd)/27 cu ft	= 0.7646 cu metre

Capacity

1 litre	= 1.7598 pt/0.8799 qt/0.22 gal
1 pint (pt)	= 0.568 litre
1 quart (qt)	= 1.137 litres
1 gallon (gal)	= 4.546 litres

Weight

1 gram (g)	= 0.035 oz
1 kilogram (kg)/1000 g	= 2.20 lb/35.2 oz
1 tonne/1000 kg	= 2204.6 lb/0.9842 ton
1 ounce (oz)	= 28.35 g
1 pound (lb)	= 0.4536 kg
1 ton	= 1016 kg

Pressure

1 gram per square metre $(g/metre^2)$	= 0.0295 oz/sq yd
1 gram per square centimetre (g/cm^2)	= 0.228 oz/sq in
1 kilogram per square centimetre (kg/cm^2)	= 14.223 lb/sq in
1 kilogram per square metre $(kg/metre^2)$	= 0.205 lb/sq ft
1 pound per square foot (lb/ft^2)	= 4.882 kg/metre^2
1 pound per square inch (lb/in^2)	= 703.07 kg/metre^2
1 ounce per square yard (oz/yd^2)	= 33.91 g/metre^2
1 ounce per square foot (oz/ft^2)	= 305.15 g/metre^2

Temperature

To convert °F to °C, subtract 32, then divide by 9 and multiply by 5
To convert °C to °F, divide by 5 and multiply by 9, then add 32

Phototypeset by Tradespools Limited, Frome, Somerset
Printed and bound by Artes Gráficas, Toledo, SA, Spain
D. L. TO:379-1986